Little Bluejay

AN ORIGINAL COLLECTION

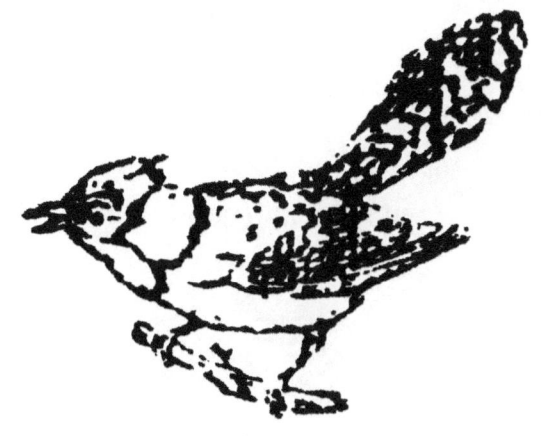

BETTY LOU HARGIS

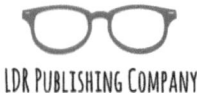
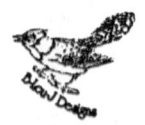

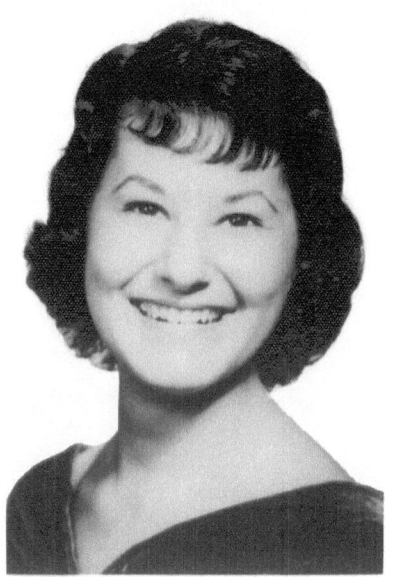

Betty Lou Hargis

Born on March 3, 1941

A wise woman once said, "Betty is original, artistic, and up-to-date on fashions. She is also business - like, prompt, and efficient. In fact, I can't think of anything that Betty doesn't do well. Wherever she goes she will be an asset to any team." Anyone who knows her well can attest to that.

It is an honor and a pleasure to showcase just a small portion of her incredible works. I present to you a collection of original poems and artwork she created. "The Little Bluejay" is appropriately named after 'B-Lou-J Designs', the signature used for her many works of art.

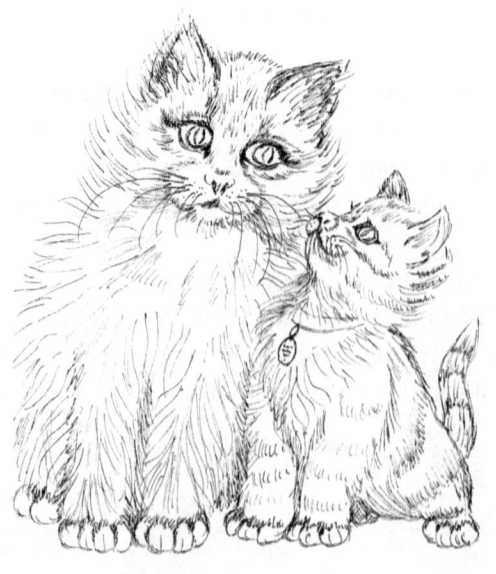

Dearest Mom and Dad,

Let me tell you about two people,
I've known since I was born.
They surrounded me with Love,
They kept me safe, they kept me warm.

You see I dearly Love them,
More than my very life.
Yet at times I have hurt them,
And for this I must pay the price.

My sorrow it runs deeply,
For the hurt that I have caused.
Forever can't erase it,
Nor can it be truly lost.

I want to say, "I'm sorry,"
But that seems so small and meek.
I hope they can forgive me,
Their child who is so weak.

The gifts -- there are so many --
They have given me over the years.
The most precious one I will tell you,
If I can only hold back the tears.

They taught me about Lord Jesus,
And His Father, God above;
About Mary, the Virgin Mother;
And of their eternal Love.

Now this lesson it has given me,
Joy I can't explain,
And I pray that it can help them,
In the forgiving of the pain.

Thank you, God, for giving me,
These people in my life;
My Mother and my Father,
Without them, what is life?

I pray one day my children,
Will Love God as I do.
For this would be a tribute,
To Mom and Dad... I Thank You.

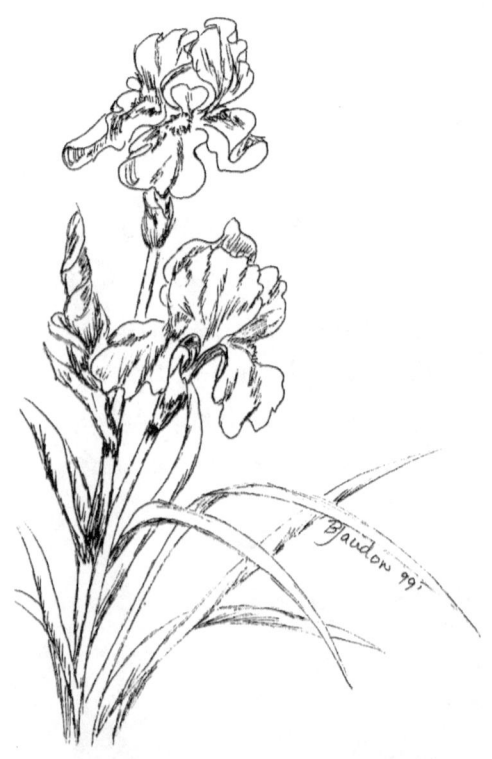

Spring

Bjaudon

April Is Finally Here
April 1, 2009

It's a laugh or a pout to the fools of the day.
April the first or last to come out to play.
Take it on the chin or conjure your own.
Bring your quip and a laugh for the fun.

April brings more sun, a bloom and the wind.
I wish you a sweet good morning rain.
Good coffee and great fellowship makes it just right.
But I'll have my own foolish joke by the end of the night.

April Fool!

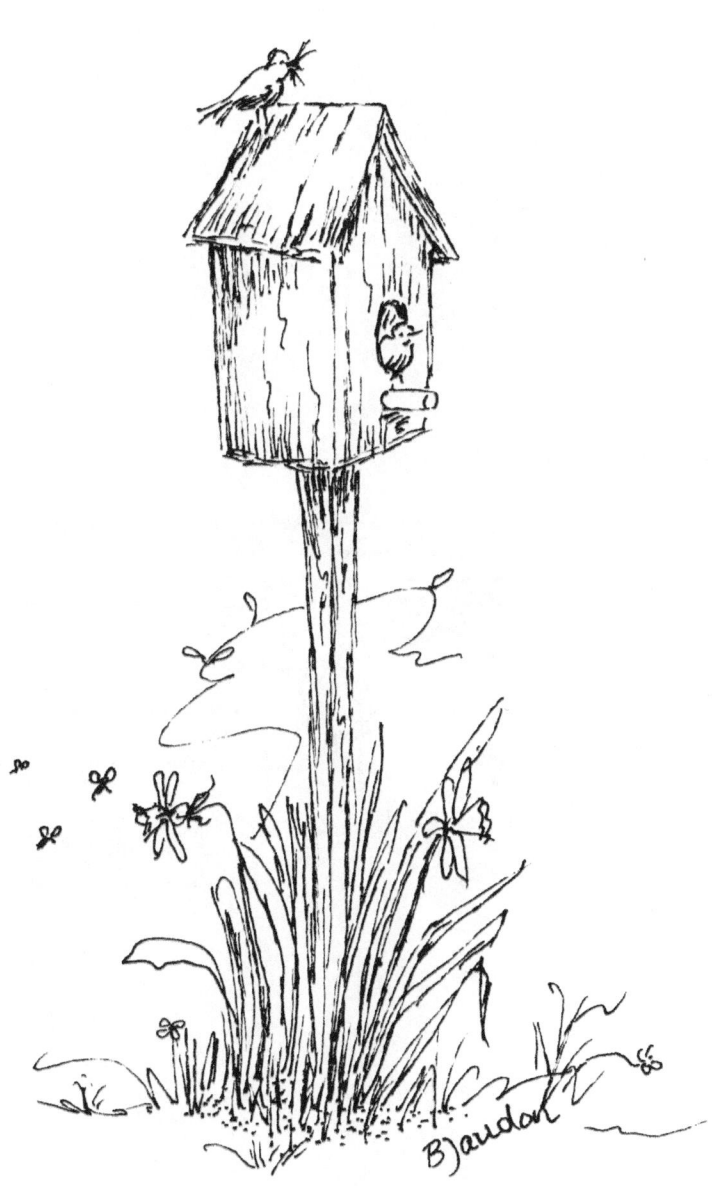

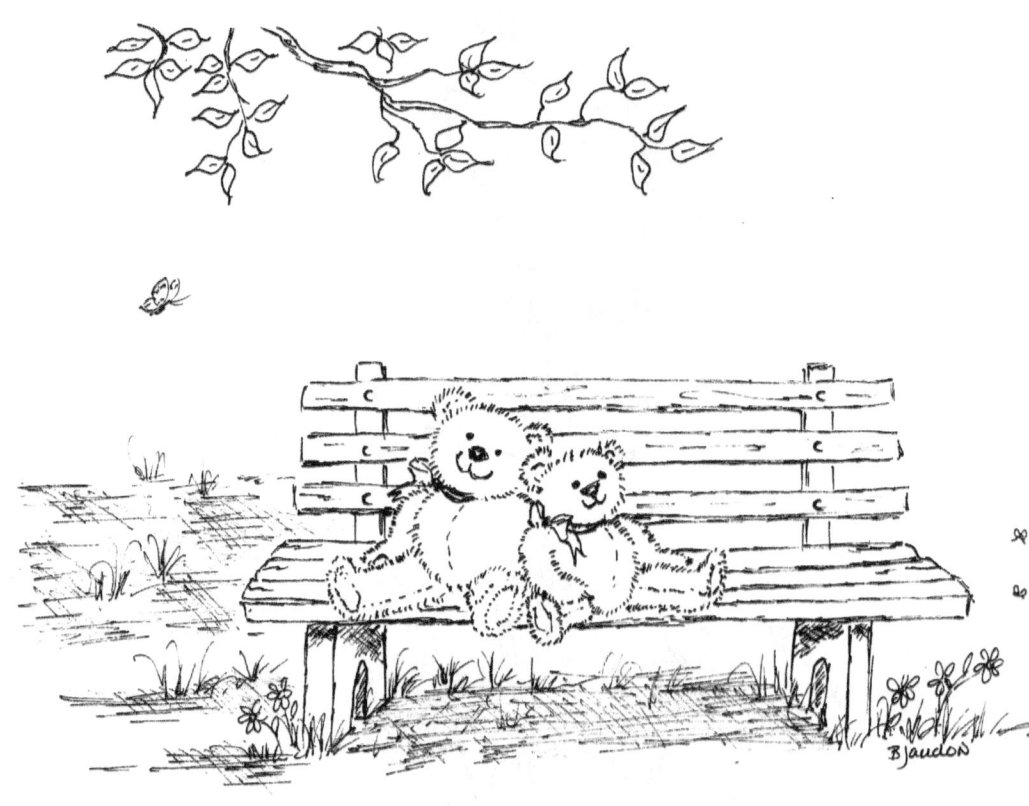

Friendship

If I could catch a rainbow.
I would do it just for you.
And share with you its beauty.
On the days you're feeling blue.

If I could build a mountain.
You could call your very own.
A place to find serenity.
A place to be alone.

If I could take your troubles.
I would toss them in the sea.
But all these things I'm finding.
Are impossible for me.

I cannot build a mountain.
Or catch a rainbow fair.
But let me be what I know best.
A friend that's always there.

New Home
August 25, 1999

Congratulations to you -
I hear you're on the move.
To a brand new place.
At last your dreams come true.

The welcome mat says. 'COME ON IN!'
At last this house becomes the home.
Tailored for you by God above.
A special blessing on your new abode.

Your home will be filled with His Love.

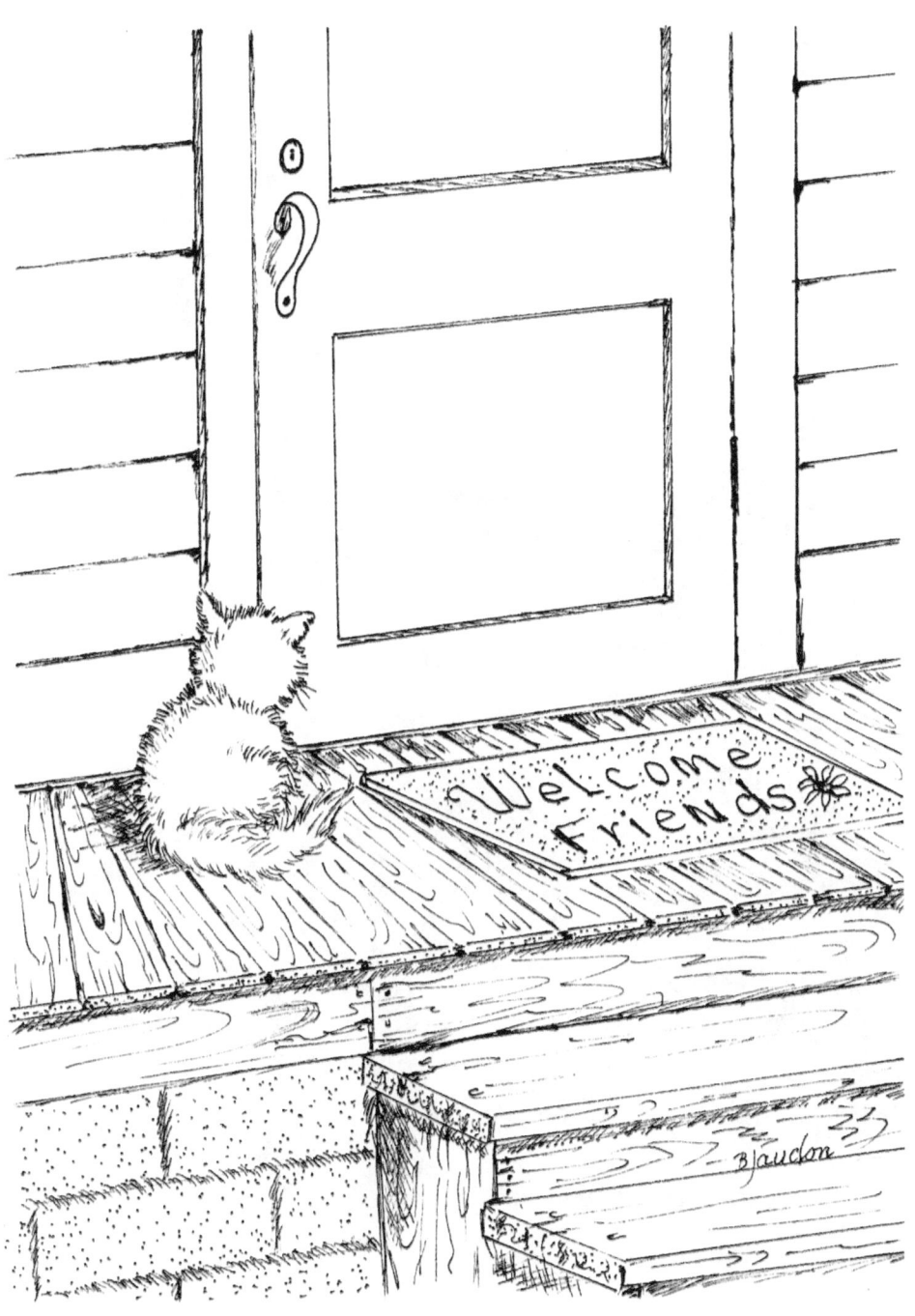

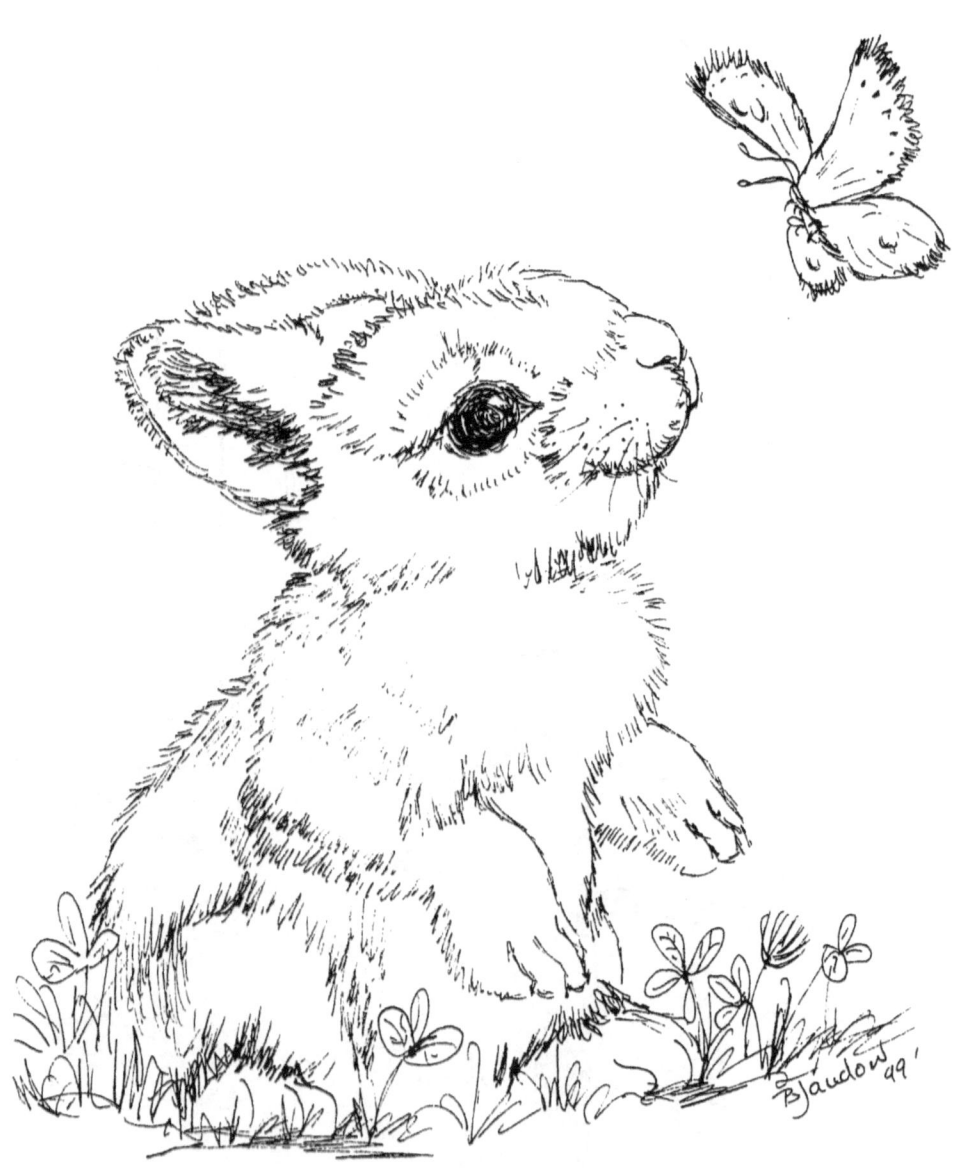

Dandy Lions
July 2010

Arising from nature's sleep they invade your space.
All the while, charming you with their yellow beauty.
Then, in a blink, into mystical balls they're transformed,
Suspended like small clouds resting on tall stems,
Readied for the final blow.

They infuriate, as a million soldiers are launched,
Playfully scattered on a puff of wind.
They drift and float before coming to rest,
Spreading their virus, again in secret places, unseen
A false friend to every young blade.

They claim your prize - you lose!
In your lovely, well-groomed garden,
Fulfilling a timeless quest, victoriously they reign.
Like a creeping stealthy lion waiting to spring,
You will see their round yellow eyes
Peeping through the green.

Little Boy

A little boy.
So lively and charming.
A tear, a smile.
Always disarming.

Two arms held high.
For Mom and Dad, too.
The hearts are won.
With Ga, Ga-Goo, Goo.

No greater prize.
In life's choicest fair.
Or more priceless jewel.
Found anywhere.

How then so blessed.
Can two people be?
Appointed Parents on.
The lovely Family Tree.

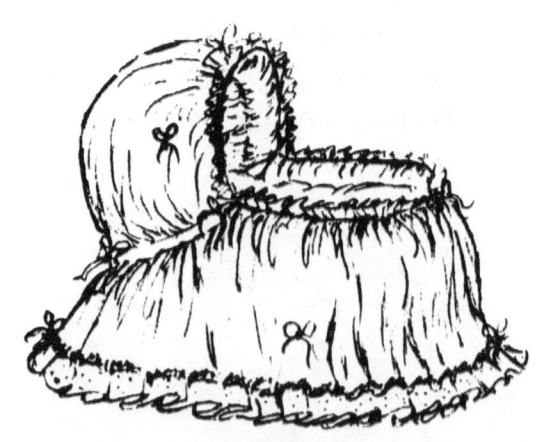

Little Girl

A little girl.
So sweet and charming.
A tear, a smile.
Always disarming.

Two arms held high.
For Papa and Nana, too.
The hearts are won.
With Ga, Ga-Goo, Goo.

No greater prize.
In life's choicest fair.
Or more priceless jewel.
Found anywhere.

How then so blessed.
Can two people be?
Appointed Grandparents' on
The lovely Family Tree.

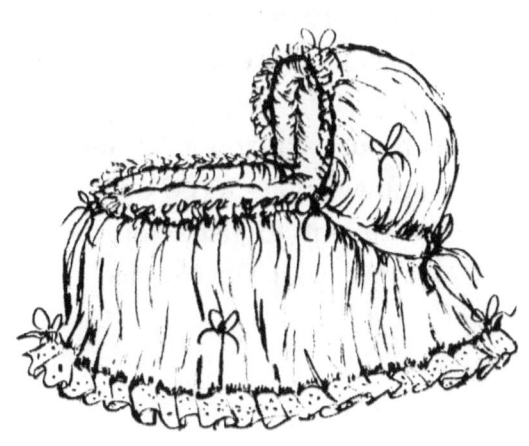

What?
April, 14, 2009

Speak a little louder.
I can't hear what you say.
Are you really laughing
Or, a little tune you play?

You look very happy.
A trophy you've just won?
The spotlight in now on you.
Tell me what have you done?

Speak up tell me your story.
I know it must be great.
You would not disturb me,
With your visit so very late.

Come now what is It?
So far you have come.
A story comes bit by bit.
I should have known.

Watch out what you listen for.
Bad news waits to be told.
It's enough to just listen.
And hear your story unfold.

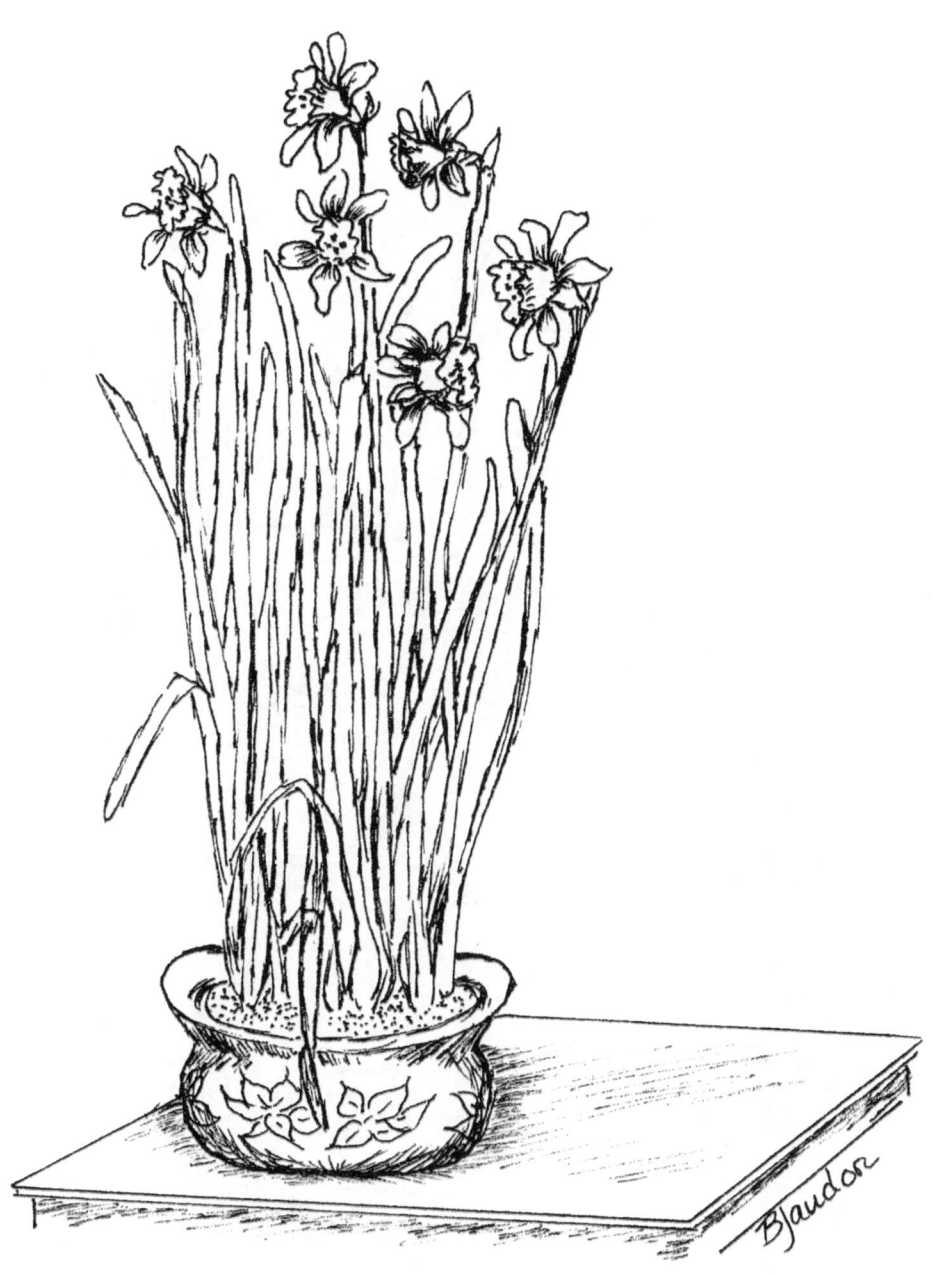

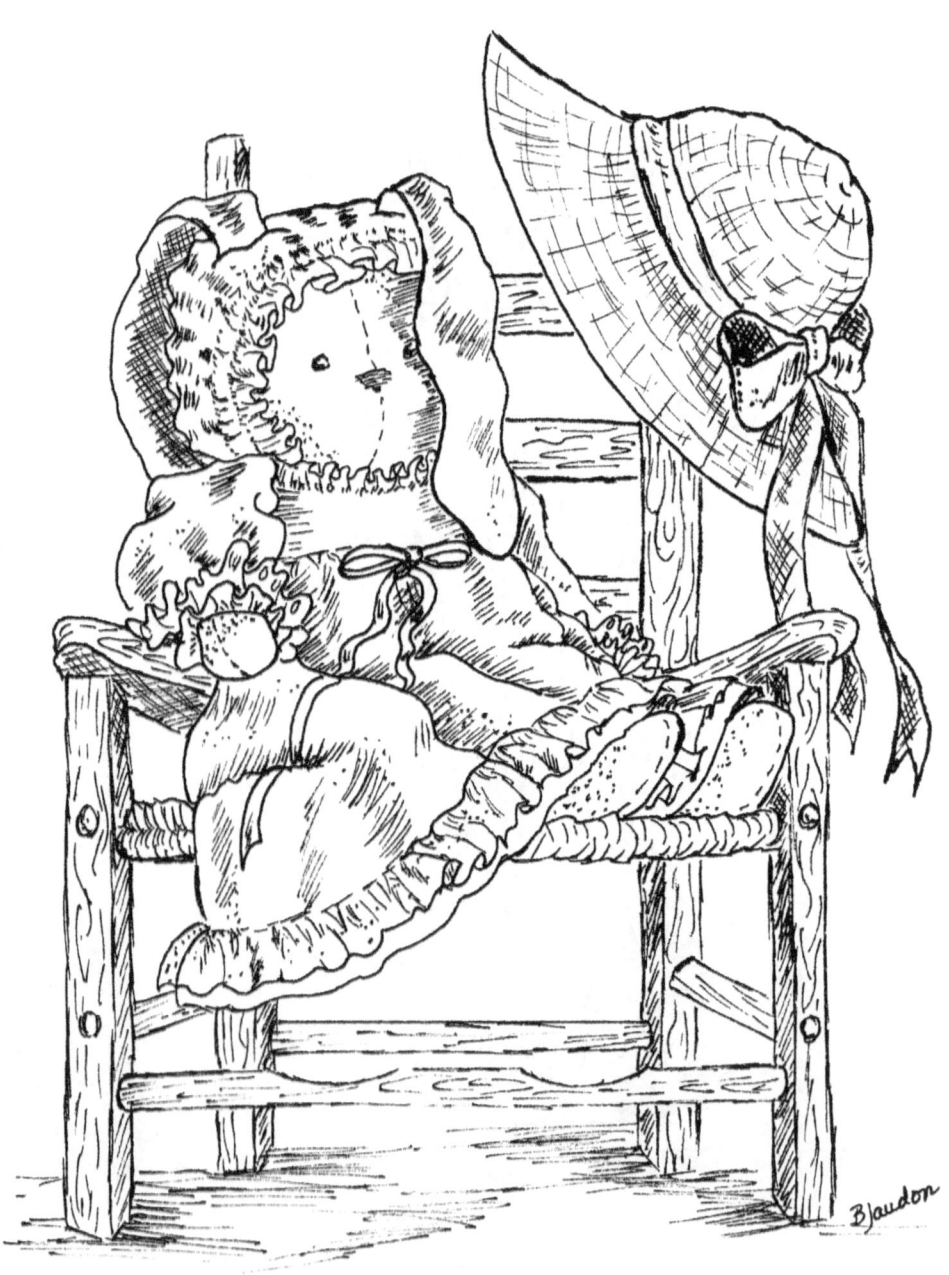

Love Story in the Rain

Hear the rain calling.
Listen to the sigh.
The rhythm tell the stories.
Of sleeping babes and lullaby's.

The words clearly glancing.
On quarrels and snarls.
Thunder and lightening.
Brave horses prancing.
Birds still their singing.
Tinkling bells keep ringing.
Trees blow bending.
Rocks smartly pelted.
Flowers and grass wilting.
Plants and trees drinking.
Animals wet coats shining.
Water falls growing.
Dark clouds billowing.
Rain on windows flowing.
Pathways flooding.
The streams are growing.
Onto light hearts dancing.
Sweethearts glancing.
Full hearts pounding.
Sweet music they hear.

A Small Voice

Hear the Voice.
Tiny whisper in the night.
So soft one must listen closely.
Or soon it will be silent

Speaks up for the Voice.
No friend can be seen.
Reluctant to be heard.
Or quick to defend.

Soon the Voice is louder.
Trying hard to be heard.
Above the foolish of clatter.
The Voice is small like a bird.

Step up front for the Voice.
Needs to be heard above all.
Let out the sounds of sadness.
Or screams will over take all.

Hear the Voice now or later.
The outcome is defined by time.
A voice soften by injustice.
Shattered by a silent crime.

Hear the small voice.
Hear the small voice.
Hear the small voice.
Hear the small voice.

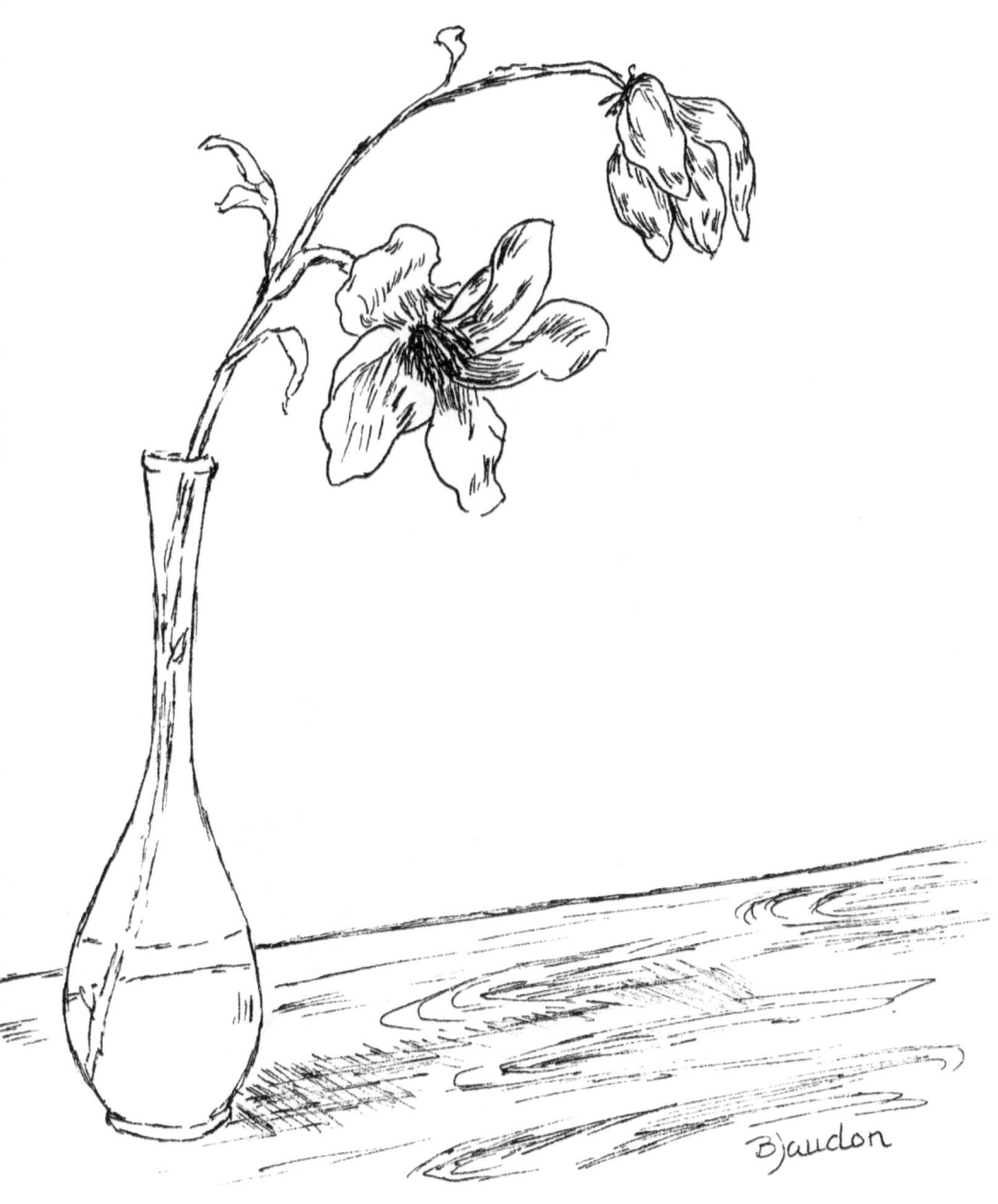

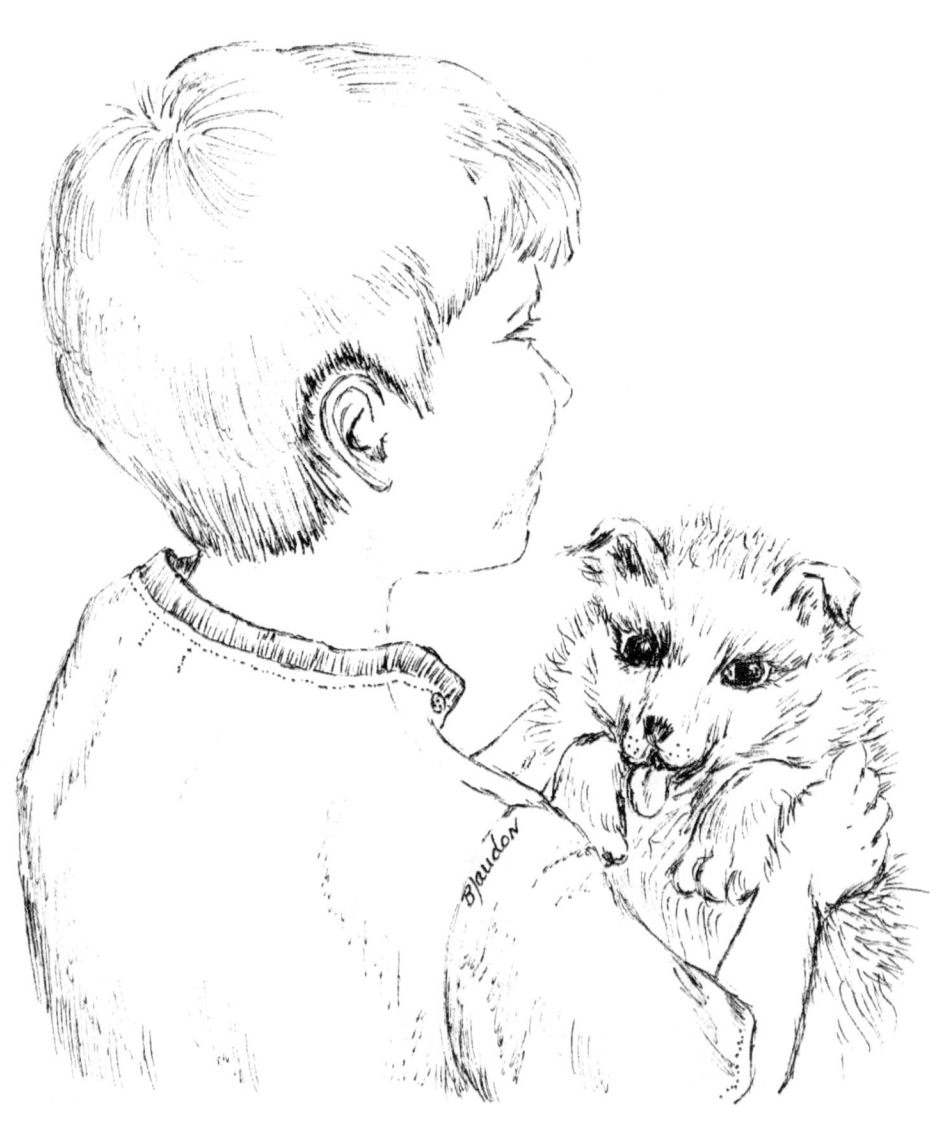

Time
April 10, 2009

Where did all the time go?
A line in a familiar song,
A question demanding an answer,
When life is almost gone.

A little late to pose the thought,
When renewal is nearly through.
Whatever we've already done,
Clearly will have to do.

In youth we find our promise,
The vast treasures of life abound.
Plant your treasure into others,
Where new life is often found.

The very best of times,
Have come and gone away.
An epitaph says a few empty lines,
Lost treasure defines our days.

Prayer

Today you are lifted up in prayer.

None of us know where the trails of life will lead.
Our hope comes with the knowledge that God goes
everywhere we go, making our path sure.
This is a deep valley but you are not there alone.

In the days ahead, you, the doctors, and your family
will be lifted in prayer.

May God bless you richly with His peace that
defies human understanding.

Today you are lifted up in prayer.

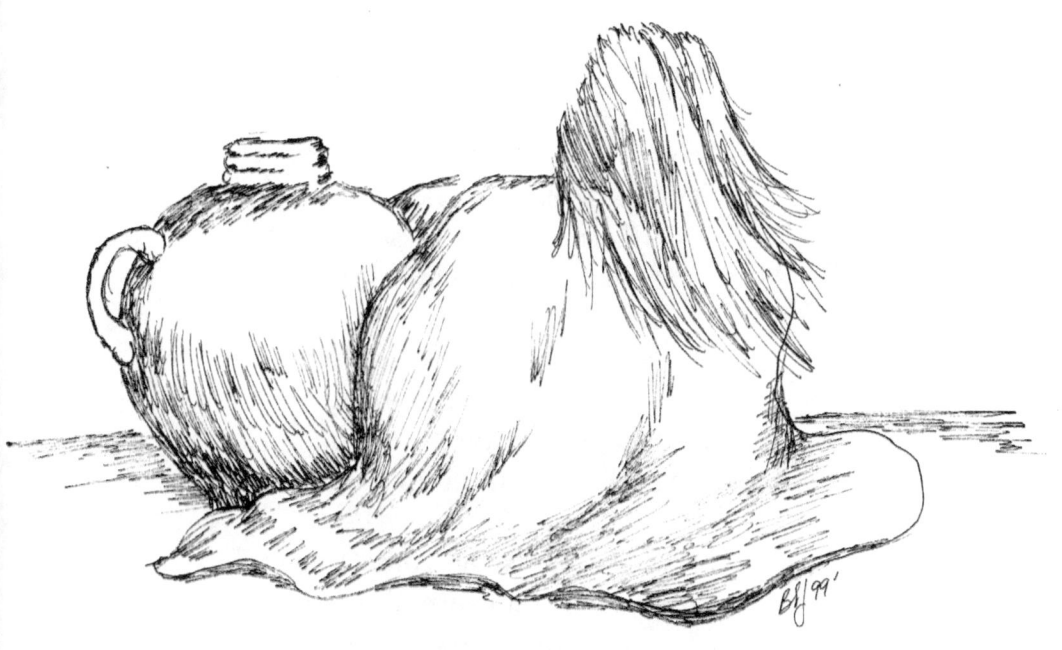

Graduation Day

A little bird has told me.
That plans are under way.
To give you some extra time.
For leisure and play.

For this day you have waited.
Meeting challenges with a smile.
Until just the right moment.
To stop and rest for a while.

Good servants rest a short spell.
Before beginning once again.
Plowing new fields of service.
New places with new plans.

I wish you wide open spaces.
No boundaries to be found.
Challenges that thrill your soul.
New ground to be plowed.

All your dreams can come true.
In the time you can now afford.
A long time you've waited.
For your future to explore.

When there is time for reflection.
On your time and service spent.
May God bless those memories.
And kindness you have lent.

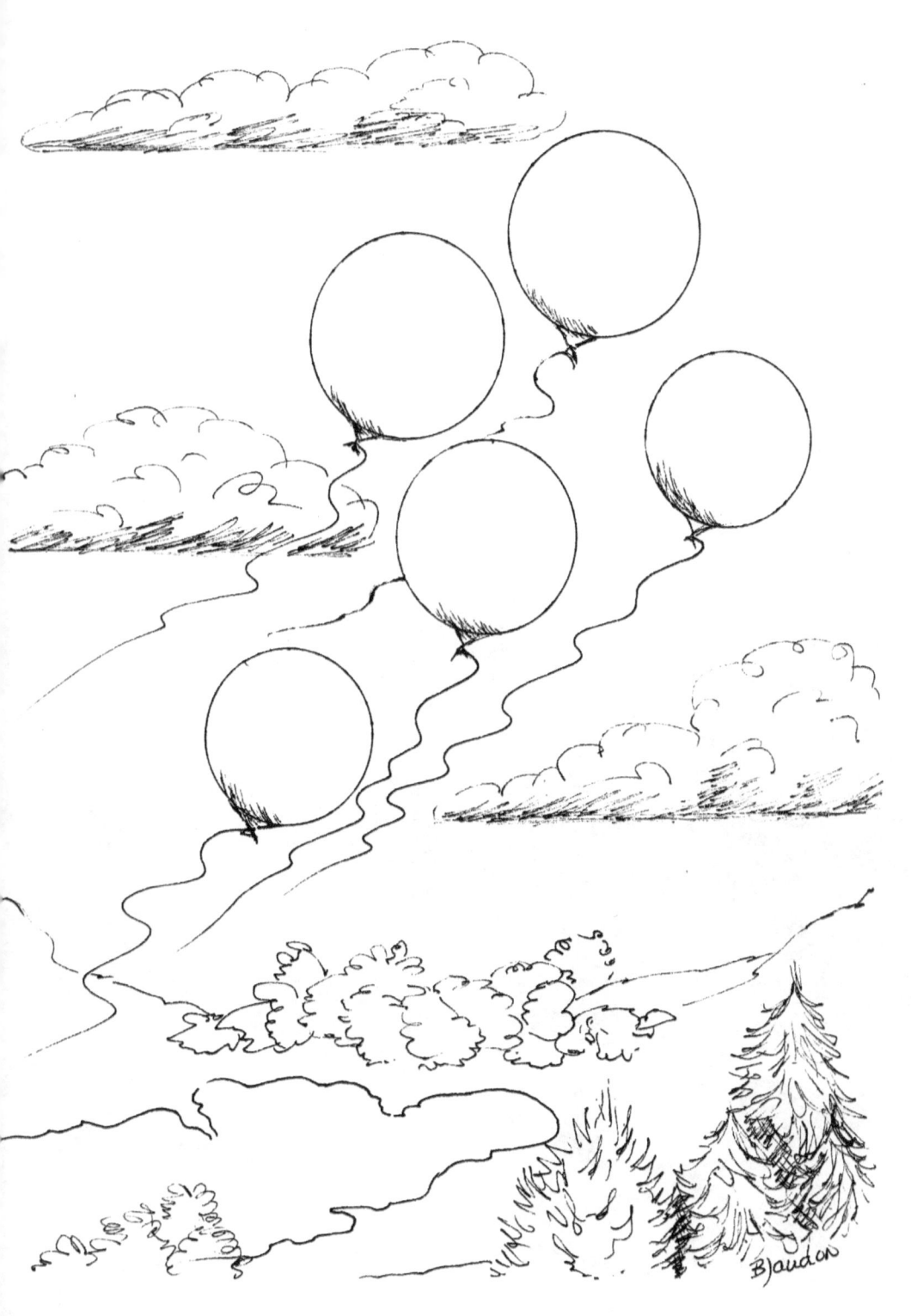

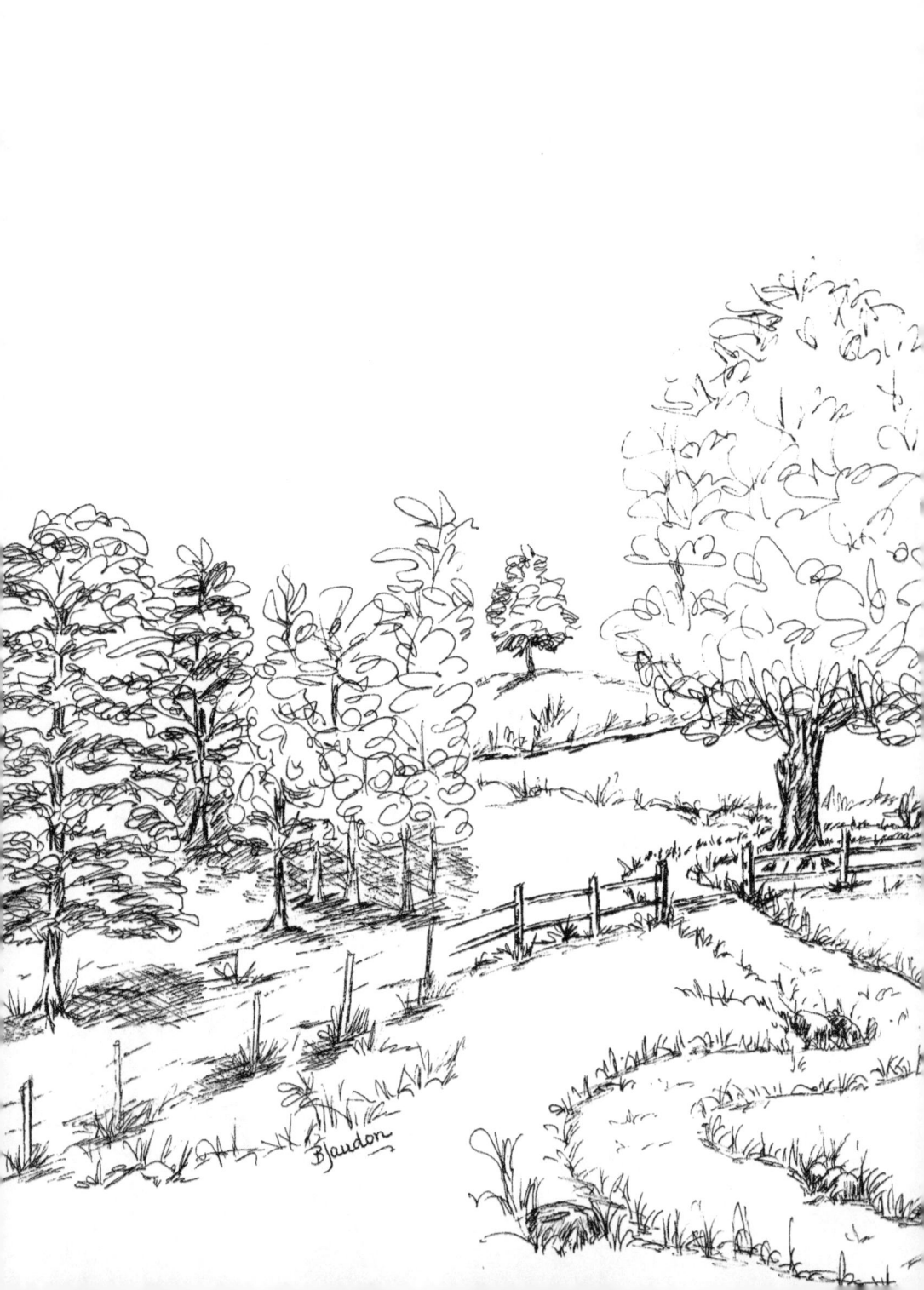

Summer

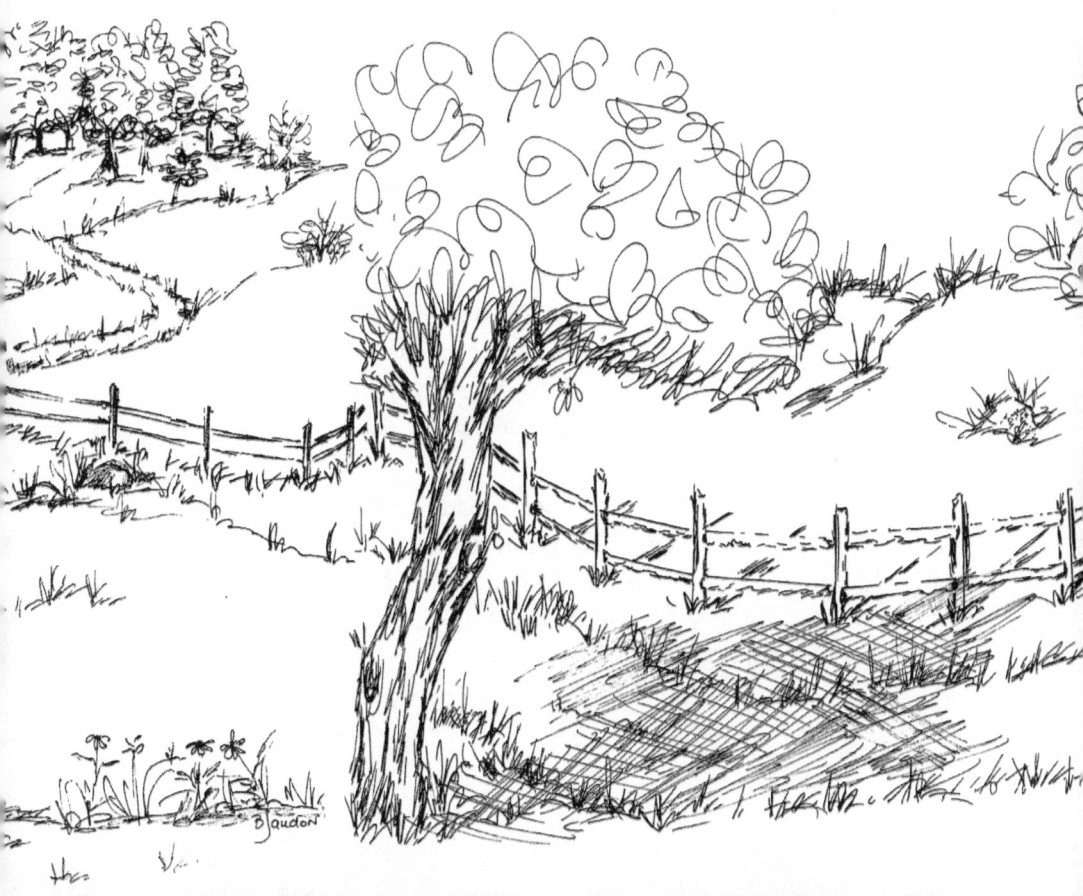

JUDY LANE POODY
June 19, 1999

J is for the JOY that comes.
From her overflowing heart.
And UNDER Jesus' blood.
She allows each day to start.

D is for the DEBT.
She feels is never ever paid.
And answers with a YES.
To a call to someones aid.

Her LOVE flows so freely.
Like a rushing mountain stream.
Her arms are ALWAYS open.
To share a wishful dream.

She NEVER leaves a little child.
Outside her longest reach.
A welcome sign to ENTER.
An opportunity to teach.

The PLAYFUL, lighthearted laughter.
Lifts up a weary soul.
And healing covers OVER pain.
Where once there was a hole.

With willing eyes wide OPEN.
To a weary travelers need.
She will DO her very best.
To plant a loving seed.

No need to look at YESTERDAY.
Her sights look forward to. .. GOD'S WAY.

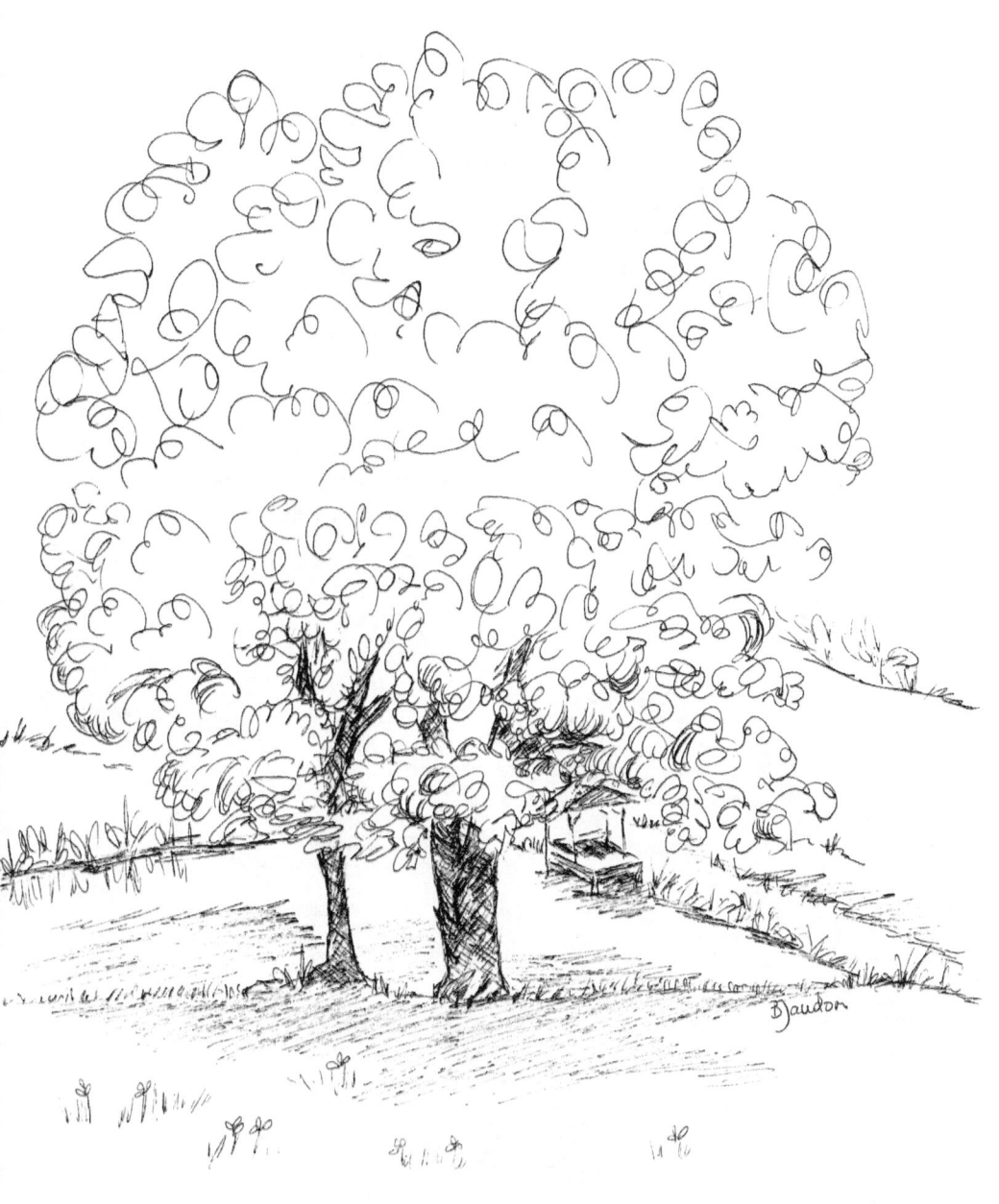

A Day at the Beach

Sink your feet into the hot, wet, sand.
Balance on one foot if you think you can.
Skip through the ocean water, kicking with your toes,
Leave watery footprints the waves will dispose.

A wave comes rushing too fast,
Covering your skin with a cool salty blast.
Your balance is lost, tumbling you go,
Giggling and laughing you submit to the flow.

A day at the beach is never wasted,
When sweet peace and power are tasted.
Savor the time spent in leisure and ponder,
God's gifts and His grace as defined in this splendor.

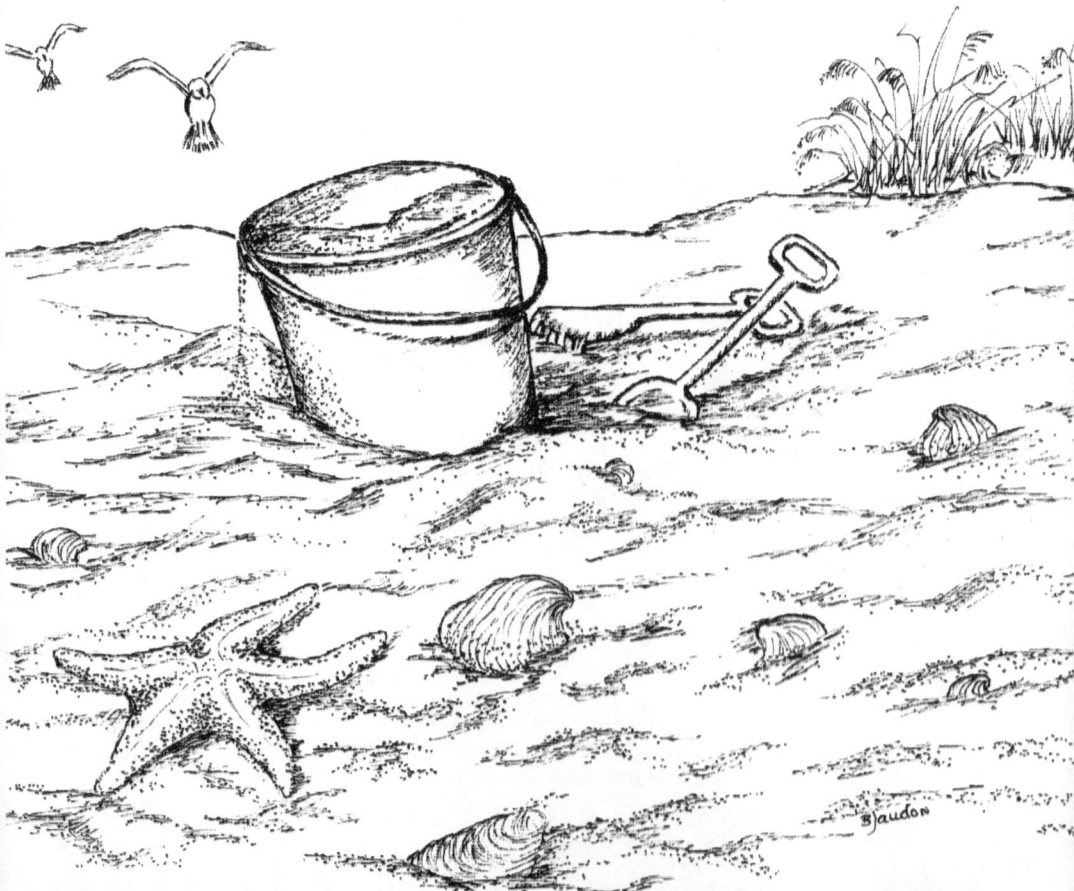

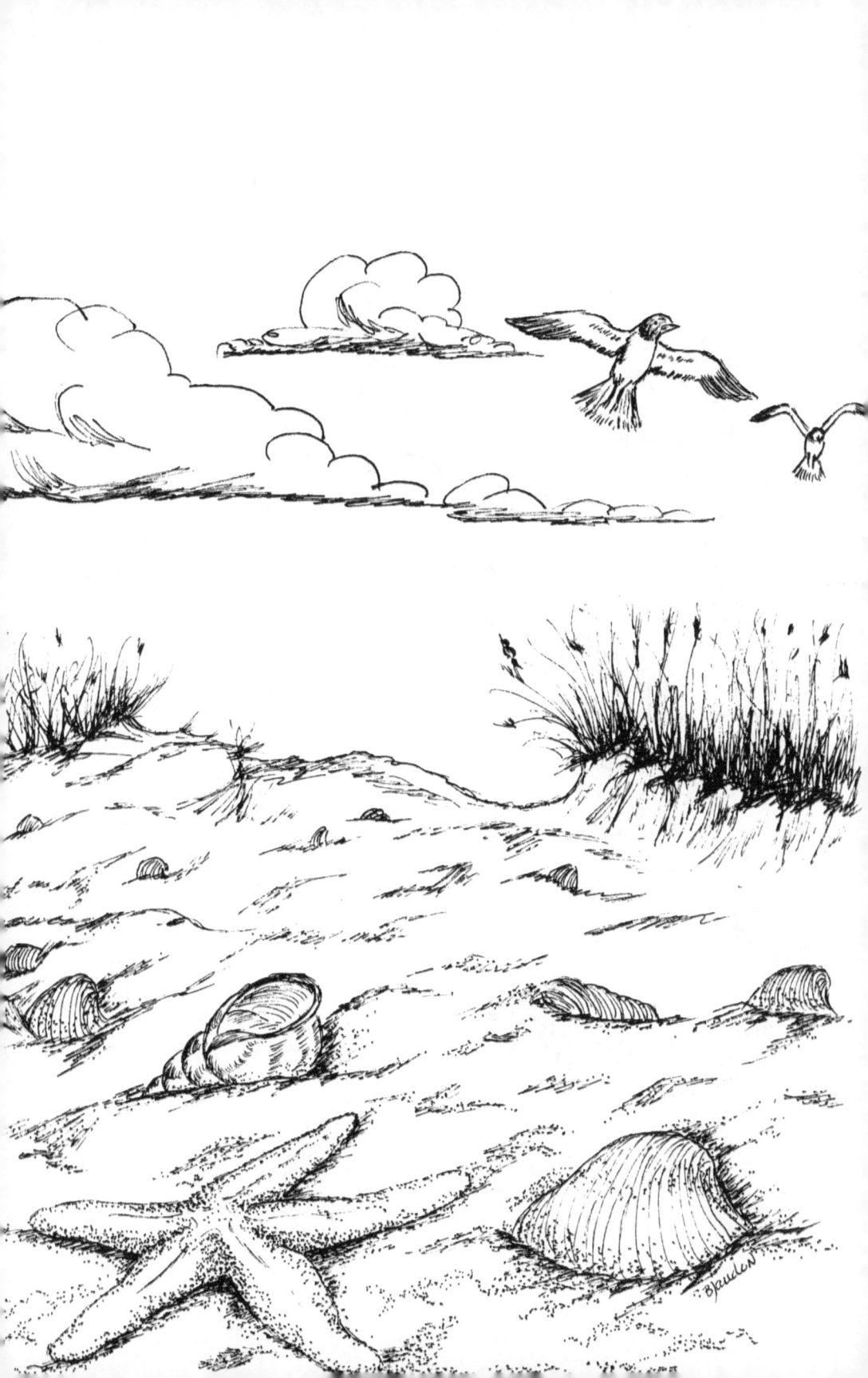

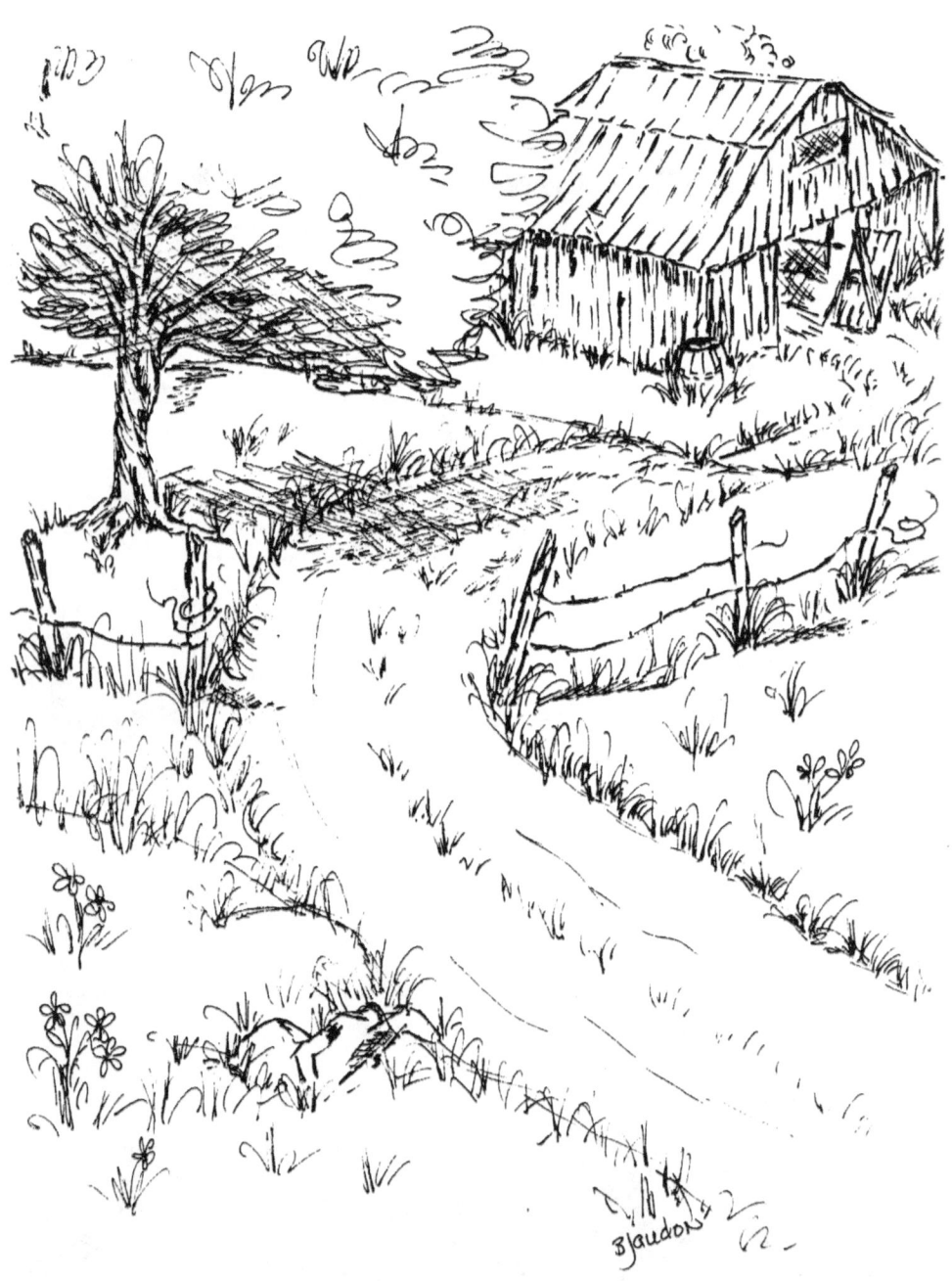

The Farmer's Hope
April 2009

Row-marks cut into fresh plowed ground:
Proof of the sage farmer's endless will.
His visible expression of hope resounds
From many years of planting skill.

His faith on the wing again will soar:
The pain from labor is no longer felt
As fields are dressed in rainbows of color
Like patchwork squares on a handmade quilt.

The farmer's hope through toil reveals
Gifts from the sun, rain, and insect wing.
Life springs abundant from the tended fields,
Supporting his ritual of hope once again.

Nature's rhythm paints a blazing scene
That will turn the key to winter's door.
A temporary end to the farmer's dream,
God's timeless promise fulfilled once more.

Hey David
June 29, 1999

You were Darling as a little boy,
Growing up a 'fix it' man.
Apple of your Mother's eye,
Playing ball and kick-the-can.
Visions dancing through your head,
Of what your life will be.
Independent of the Binion Clan,
Foot loose and fancy free.

Don't forget there is a plan,
For the man you are to be.

Kind and gentle, everyone knows,
The kind of man you are.
Isn't it the grandest plan,
God made for you so far?
Topped off with lots of talent,
Used like the Master's hands.
Creative like the Carpenter,
Who uses a Master Plan.

He made you a special guy,
I love with all my heart.
Each one of us feels that way,
And have from the very start.
Never forget that you've been blessed,
As only our God could see.
The plan for you has unfolded,
And I'm proud as I can be.

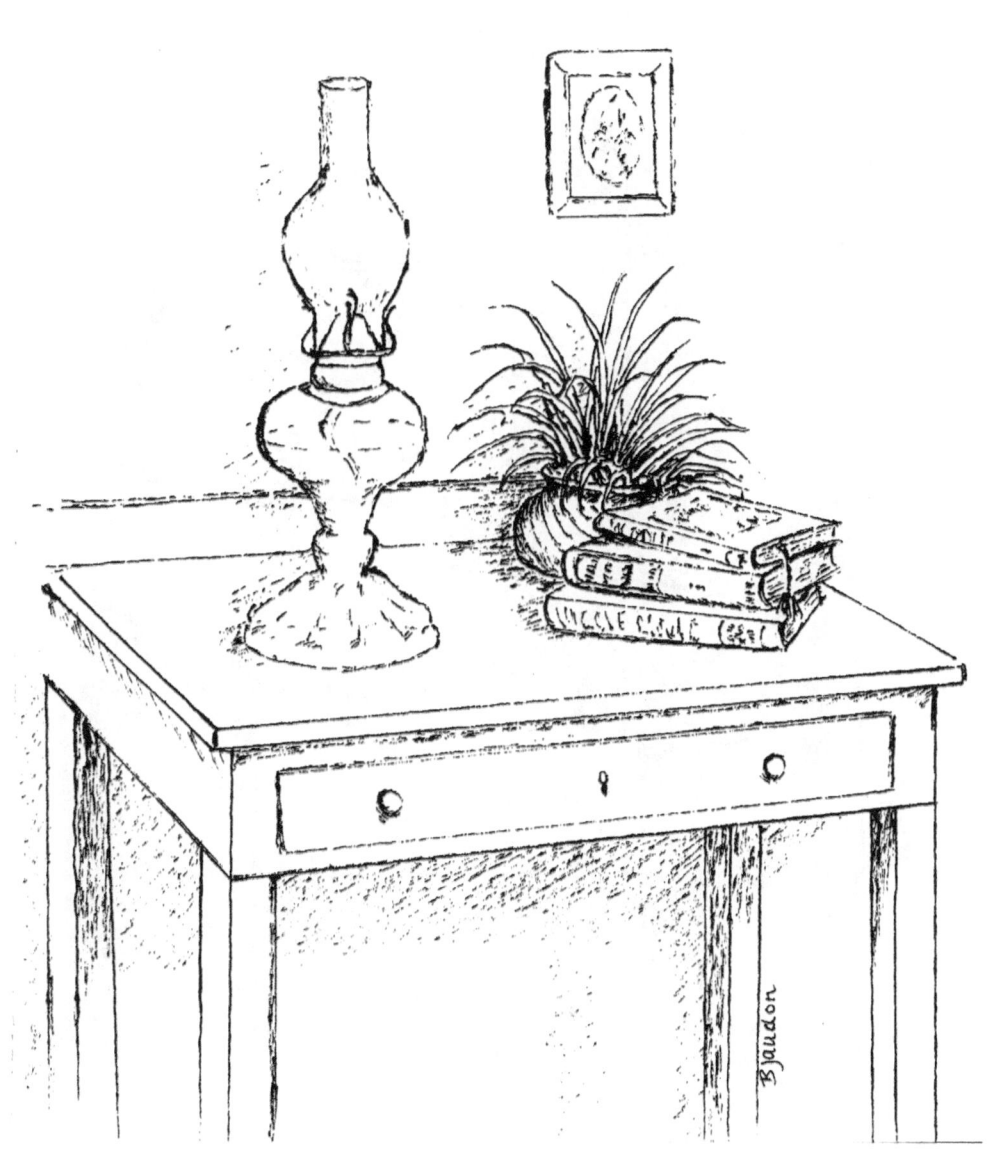

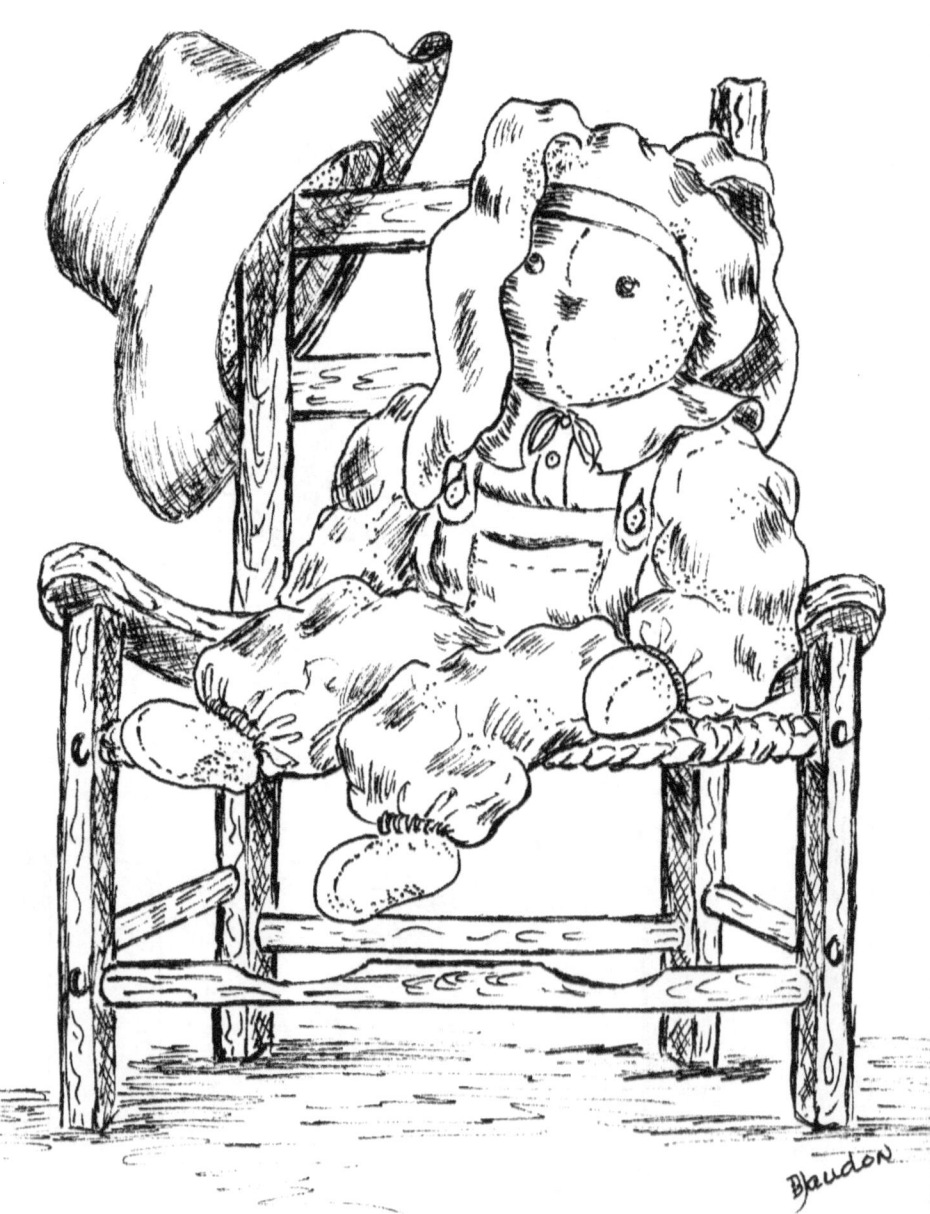

I've Heard
April, 8, 2009

I heard it said,
Or maybe I've read,
That 'nothing remains the same.'
There is comfort of thought,
That time should not,
Move us to destiny's fame.

Each child will grow,
And soon will know,
That nothing remains the same.
The youth is glad,
For fun he's had,
Something new is part his game.

Imagine your days,
Like instant replays,
No mystery part of your plan.
Life full of change,
Not easy to understand,
Rejoice! Rejoice!
Nothing remains the same.

Refreshed in nature's plan.

Life full of change,
Embrace each new day.

Decisions, Decisions
April 2009

A garden pool within my heart,
My spirit seeks time alone.
Where discovering a slower pace,
Sifting thru the daily bones.

Play forward visions lost in space.
Harsh reality falls behind,
My soul runs this peaceful place,
To the garden pool myself resign,

See there, two lanes winding,
Stretched beyond my view.
Tree lined shadows blending,
Covers which pathway to go.

In peace my spirit does wander,
Soft clouds frame my mind.
Give wings to uncertain footsteps,
Those pathways seem more defined.

I pause to inhale the horizon,
My sight is clearly restored.
No longer lost in confusion,
Assured I will choose the right door.

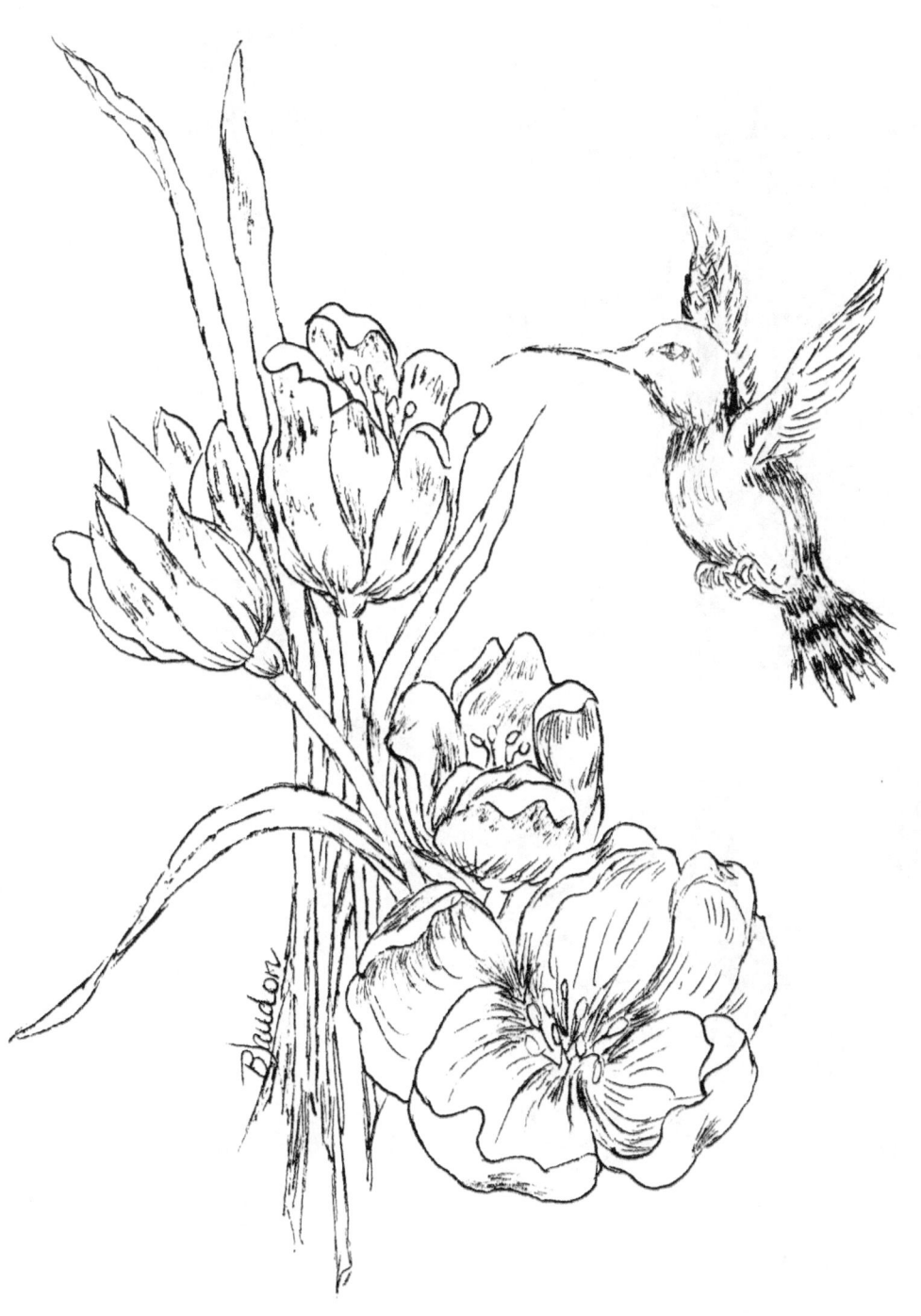

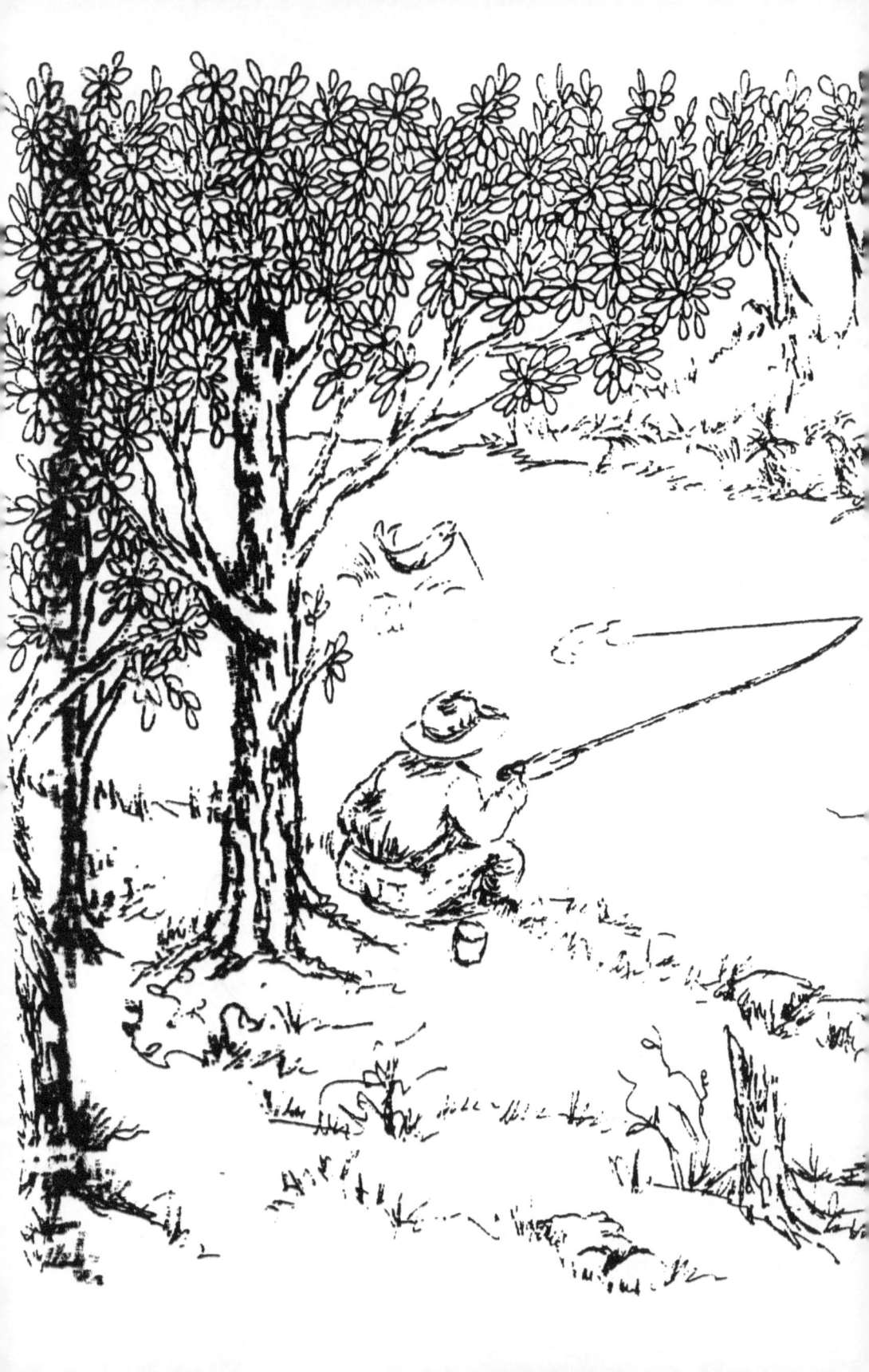

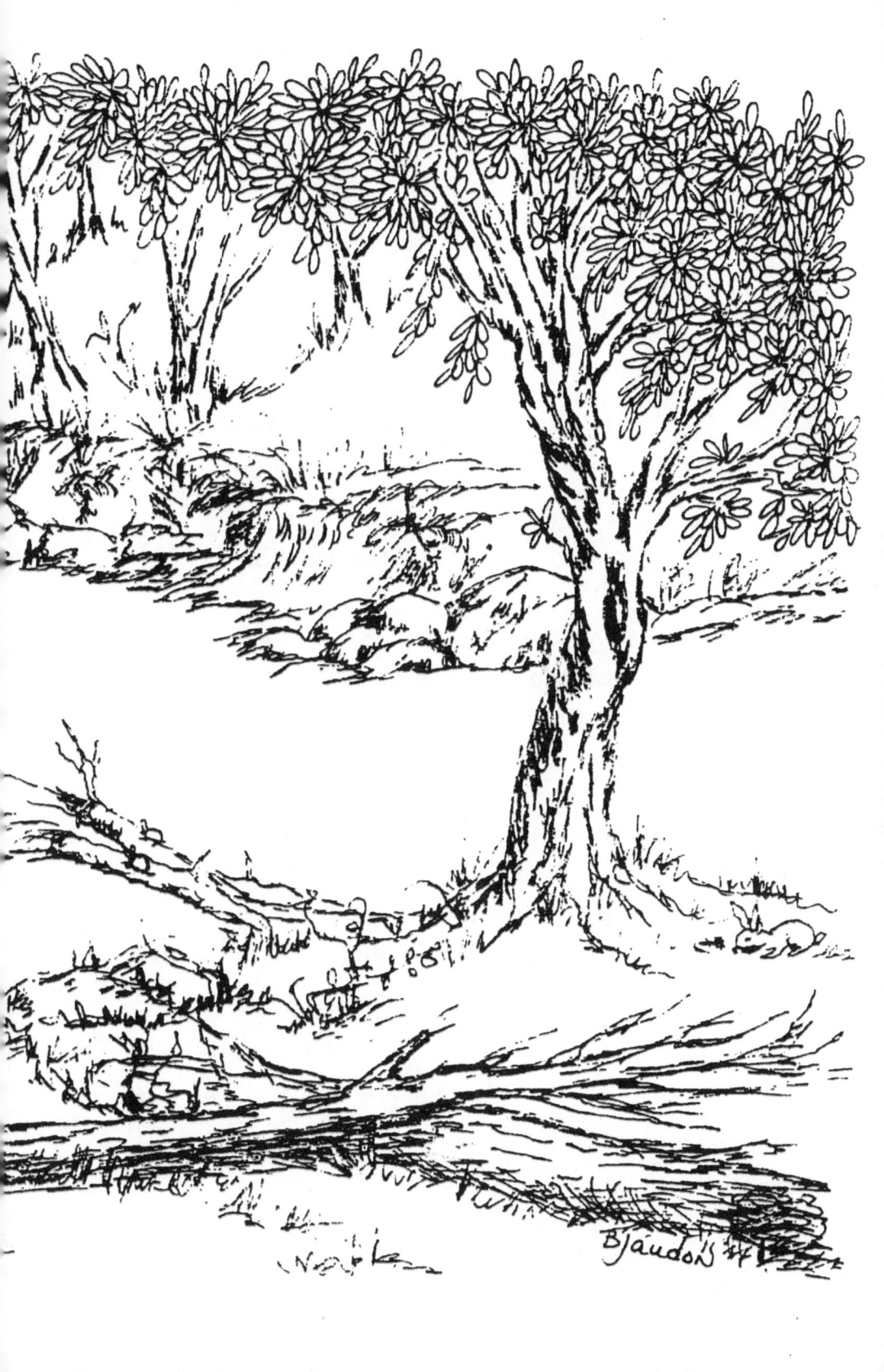

Dad's Gone Fishing

September 2008
(In memory of my Dad, Arthur Binion,
an avid creek bank fisherman)

He takes a familiar walk to.

A quiet place not easily found,
Strolling the path on leafy ground.
A time to rest the cluttered mind,
And leave the cares of the day behind.

Sit for a while at the cool, water's edge.
Watch shadows play to the wavy image.
Drop in a line-the expectations unsure,
Until, the bob of the pole and a jerk on the lure.

Through his hands, to pole and into the deep,
The cares of his world miraculously leap.
He plays with the fish that pulls at his hand,
Simpler concerns become a demand.

A joy returns to the heart and the soul,
A natural cure supplied from a pole.
Unburdens the mind from every care,
Replaced by a challenge at the end of the lure.

Dad's Gone Fishing.

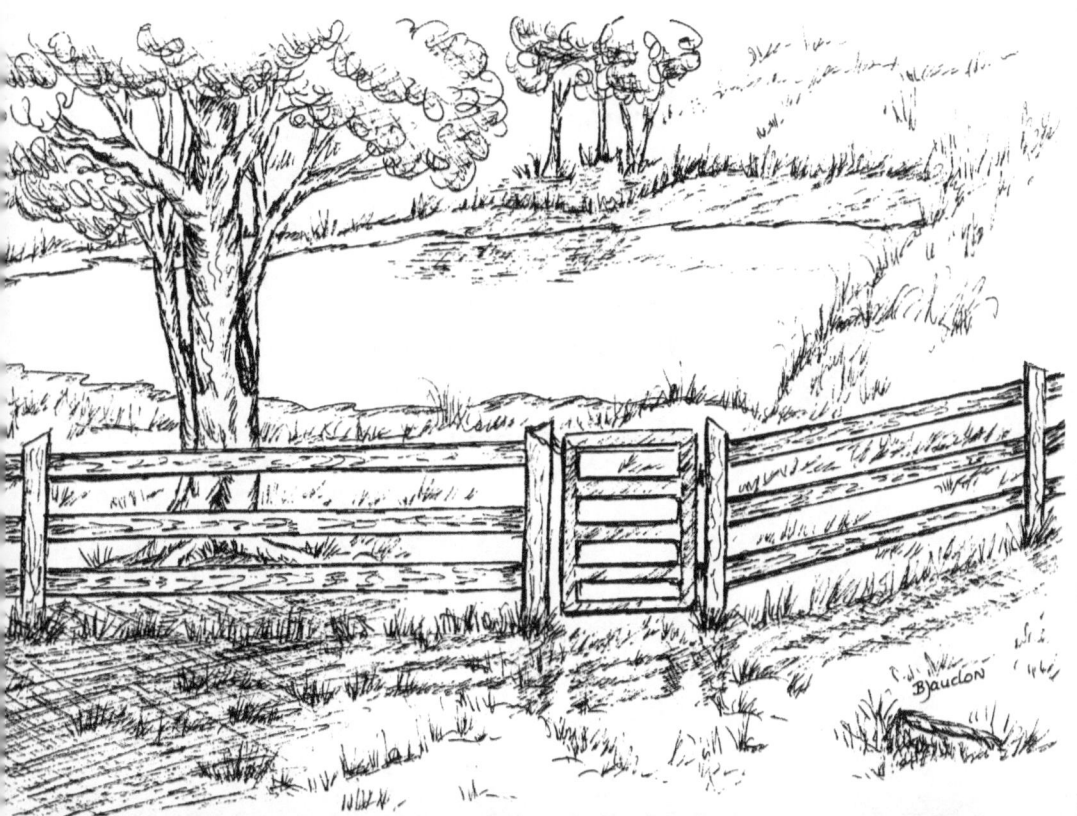

Missing You Friend

Your arms are all tired
And your voice is now weak.
The day camp demanding
As quiet time you seek.

These days without email
Makes my workdays blue.
So hurry back online
With a long note from you.

I miss all the news
Your quick notes contain.
Mine on the airwaves
Just aren't the same.

As soon as you finish,
The hard work you do.
I'll tell about 'R-2'
If you tell about 'D-too.'

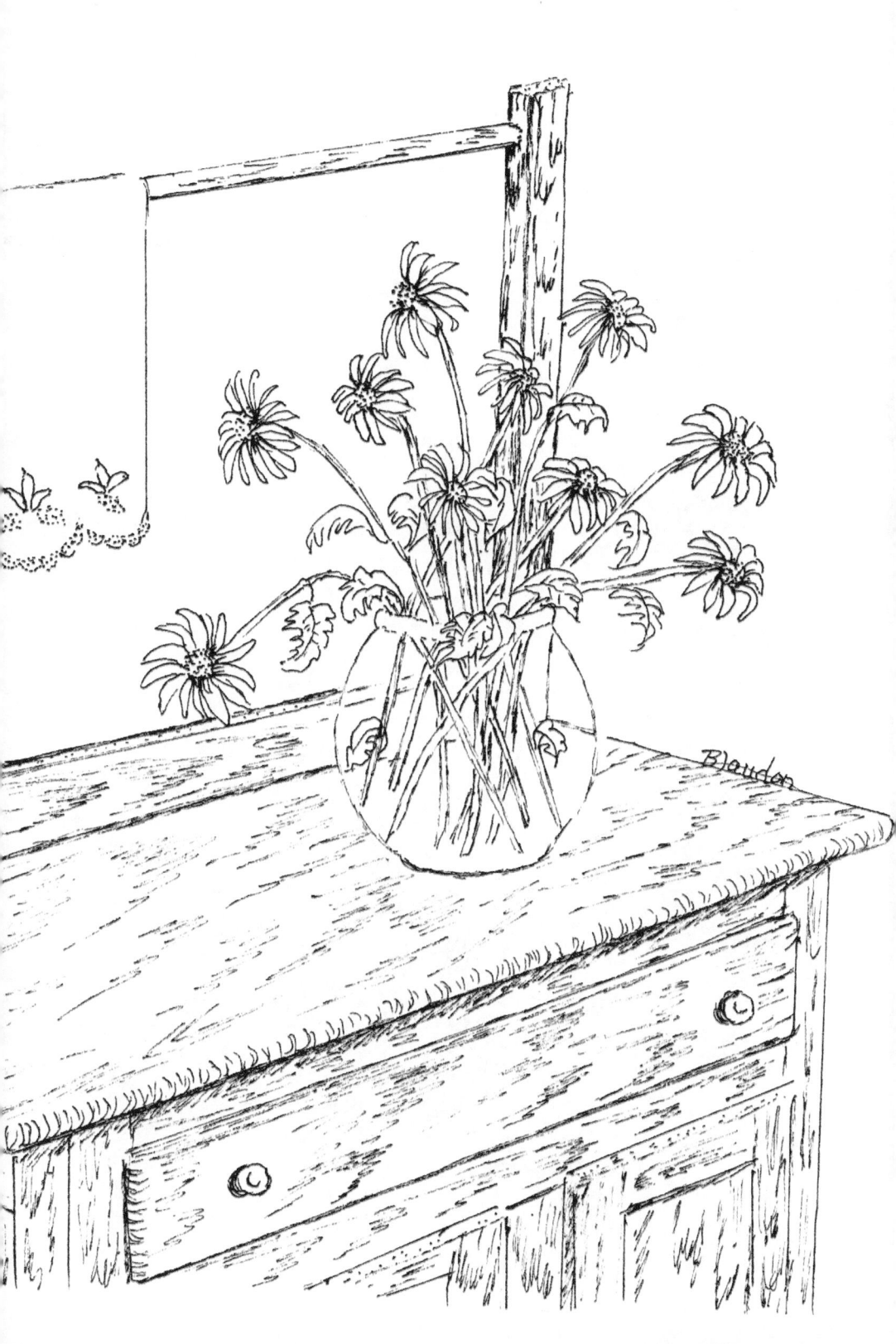

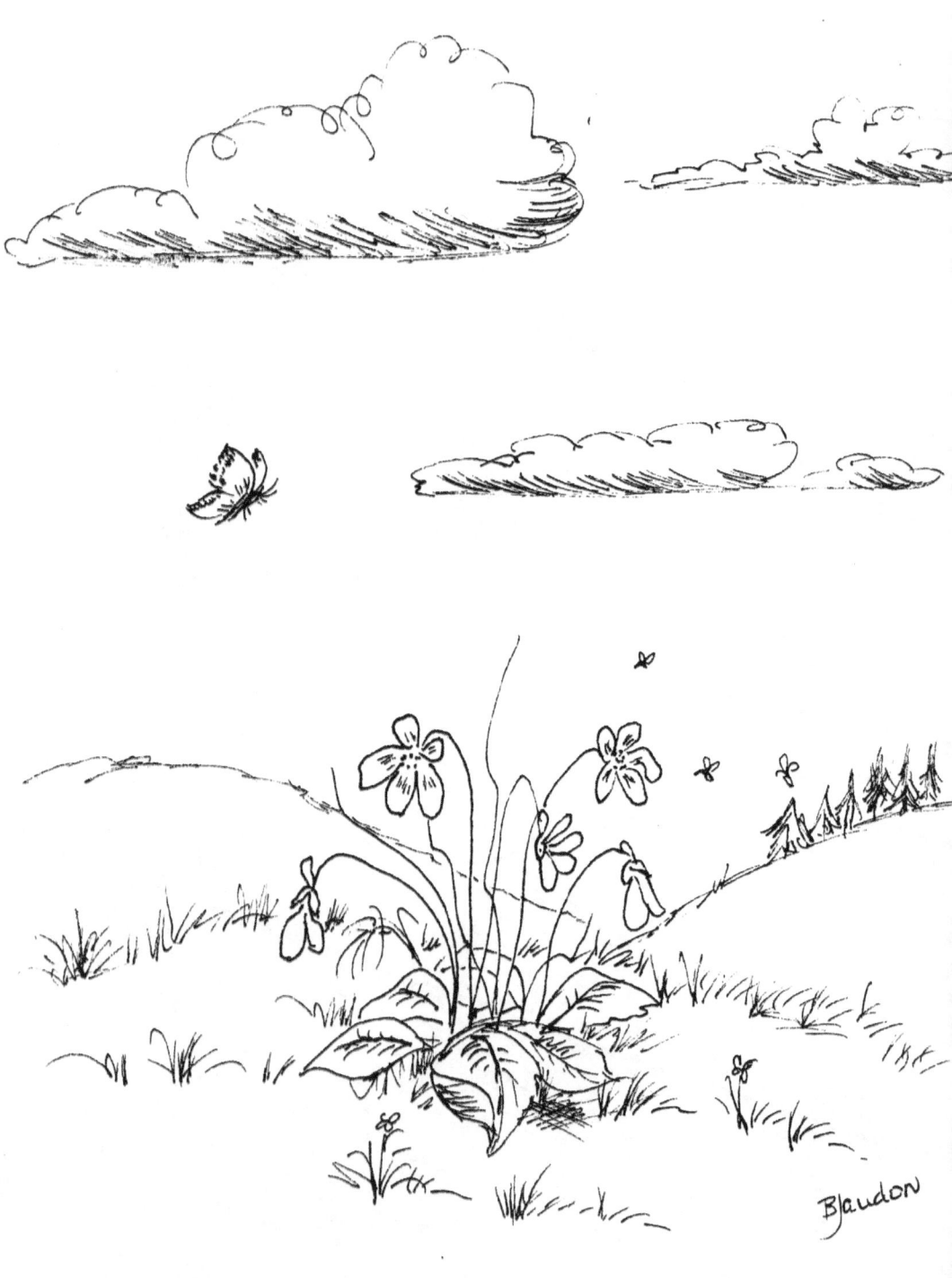

I Needed You Today

I am having for
No apparent reason,
An all together,
Yucky, sad.
Sunshine, perfect day.
Which I cannot explain,
Except by the tears,
That seems to come from
Someplace else.
So your sweet message,
Was very timely and
Encouraging and
A perfect reminder that,
All things are in the
Strong hands of our
Precious Lord.
You probably
Understand
This kind of day, too.
Thank you my friend.

Ode to Friend Judy
July 17, 1999

June was the last time.
I sent you a special card.
Unnecessary, you told me.
So please disregard.

Day 17 in July.
I'll try to jot that down.
You don't want a repeat
When your birthday rolls around.

To remember isn't easy,
At this point in time.
I put a string on my finger,
As I try to make this rhyme.

Delighted I will be,
When I do get it right.
Want my good friend to know,
The big day is in sight.

Each friend will remember,
Much more than you care.
Lost items you'll look for,
But they won't be there.

Live it up if you can
While there is still time.
The other side of this mountain
Is much harder to climb.

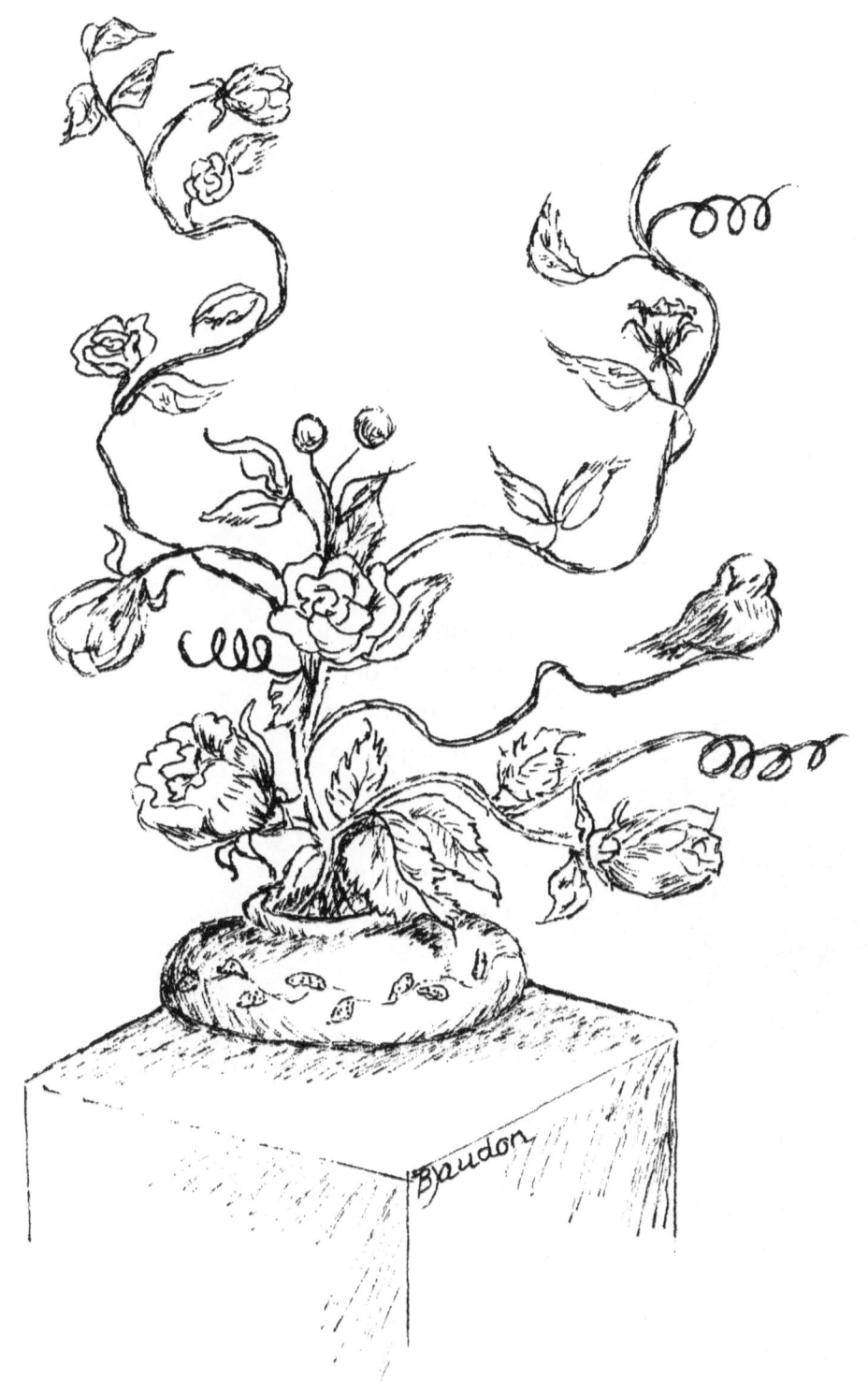

An Ordinary Life

I may leave,
My routine place
Far below
Wounded expectations,
Flee to explore
A faster pace,
Alive only in
My imagination.

Refresh my spirit,
Long run dry,
Open my heart
To anticipation,
Embrace the magic
Of life on the fly,
Finding more
Glamorous destinations.

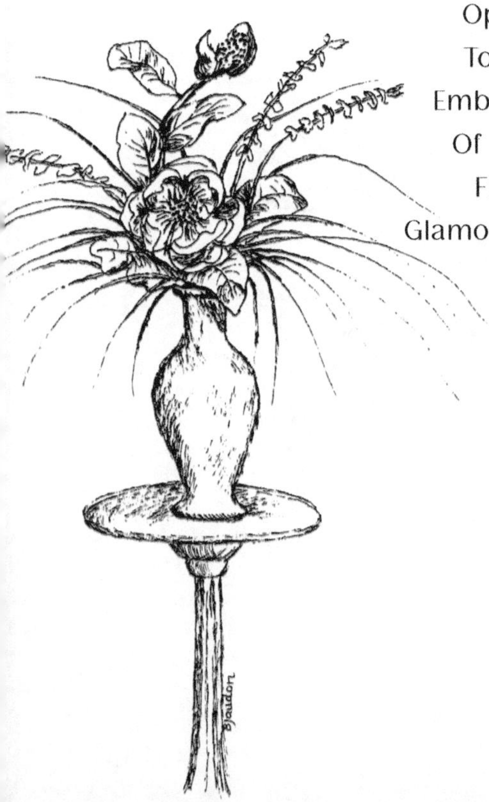

Opportunities came,
Within my reach, hesitated,
They soon fade away,
Had I claimed them
While new and fresh,
A different life
Would be mine today.

This extraordinary life,
Thus set into motion,
Ordained tomorrows
Already staged,
Equal days heaped
In pain and devotion,
Ordinary grows into
Wisdom and age.

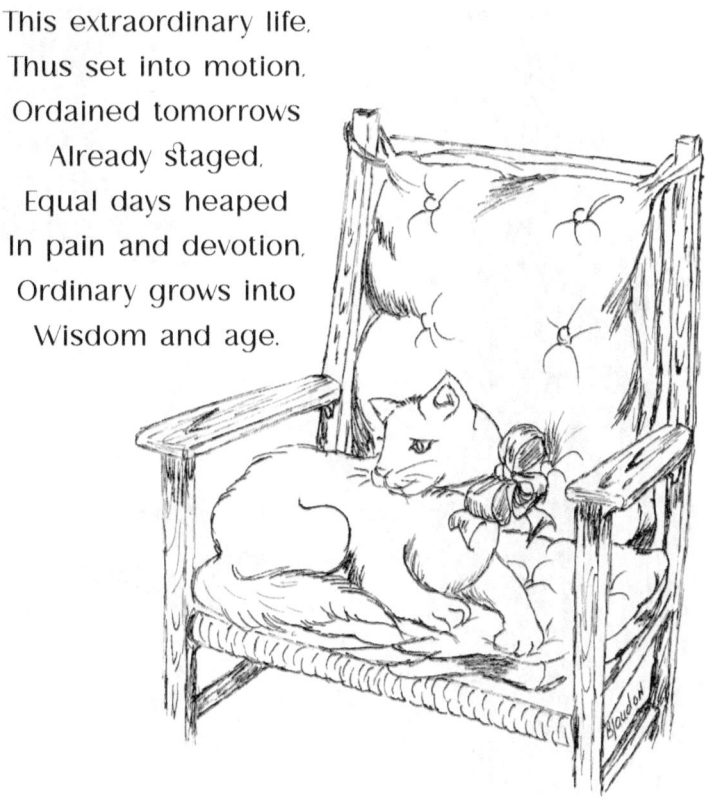

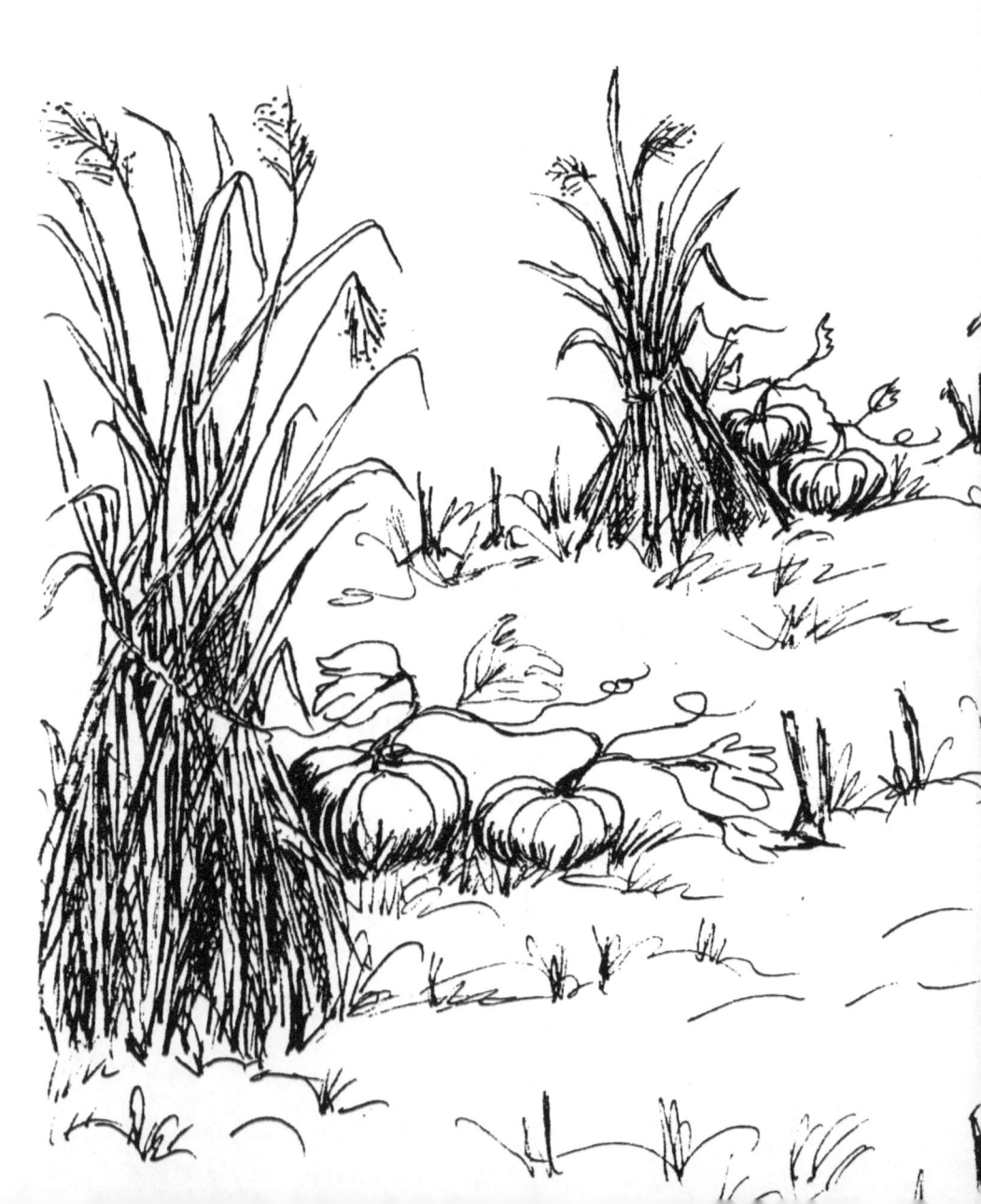

Fall

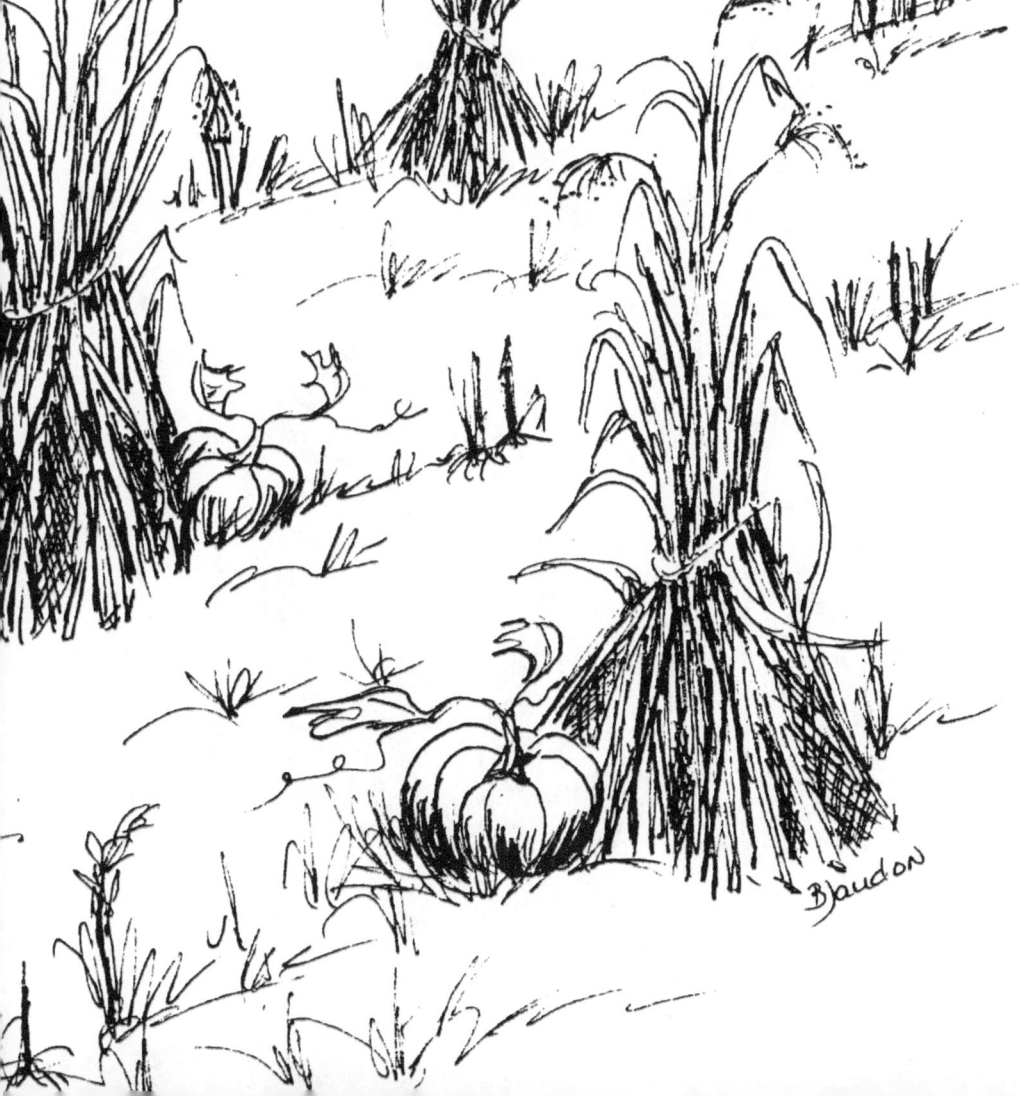

Baudon

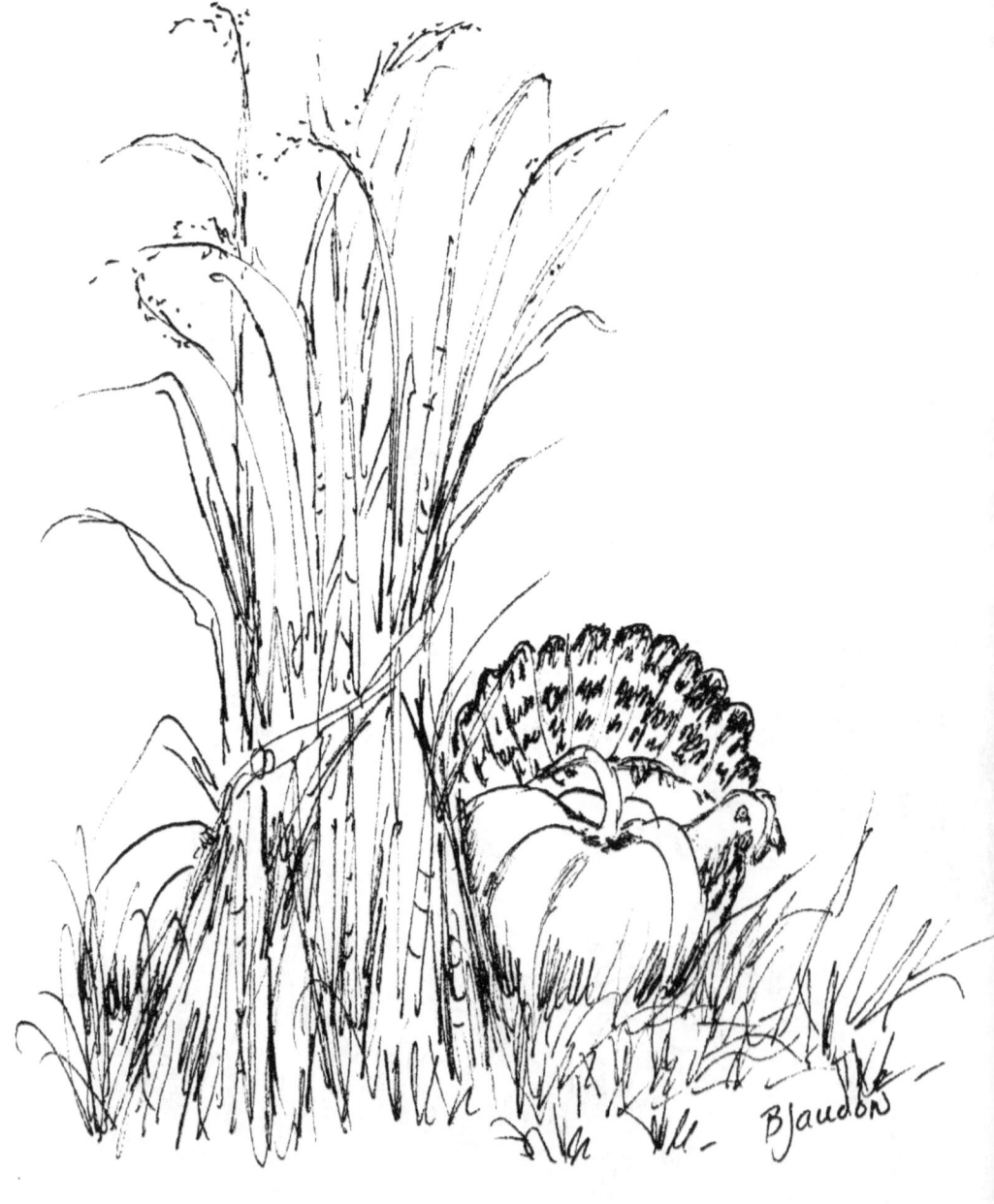

Harvest

The wind plays a rustling tune.
With the grasses oh. so dry.
The smells of the season in the air.
Drift on the leaves floating by.

Harvest time has come and gone.
The corn stalks stand up tall.
And summertime has turned into.
The glory of a golden Fall.

The fields again stand empty.
Each row. the slightest hint.
Of crops now in the pantry.
The farmers time long spent.

The new pumpkins are ripened.
All ready to be claimed.
Carved into orange glaring faces.
Lighted by a yellow flame.

Each season has its moment.
Offering joy along the way.
Painted by the Master's brush.
His Glory is on display.

THE CLASS OF 1959

So glad to be included.
In the Class of '59.
To celebrate 40 years.
Of the passing of time.

We each followed a path.
We call our destiny.
The path became the map.
Of the future we could not see.

What fun playing 'guess who?'
While peeking to read the name.
Finding that one remembered.
And learn their 'Claim-to-Fame.'

Now the party is over.
We return to our own life plan.
Glad for the time together.
Renewed friendships once again.

The time gap is narrowed.
A new memory is filed away.
Each one remembered forever.
The way we are today.

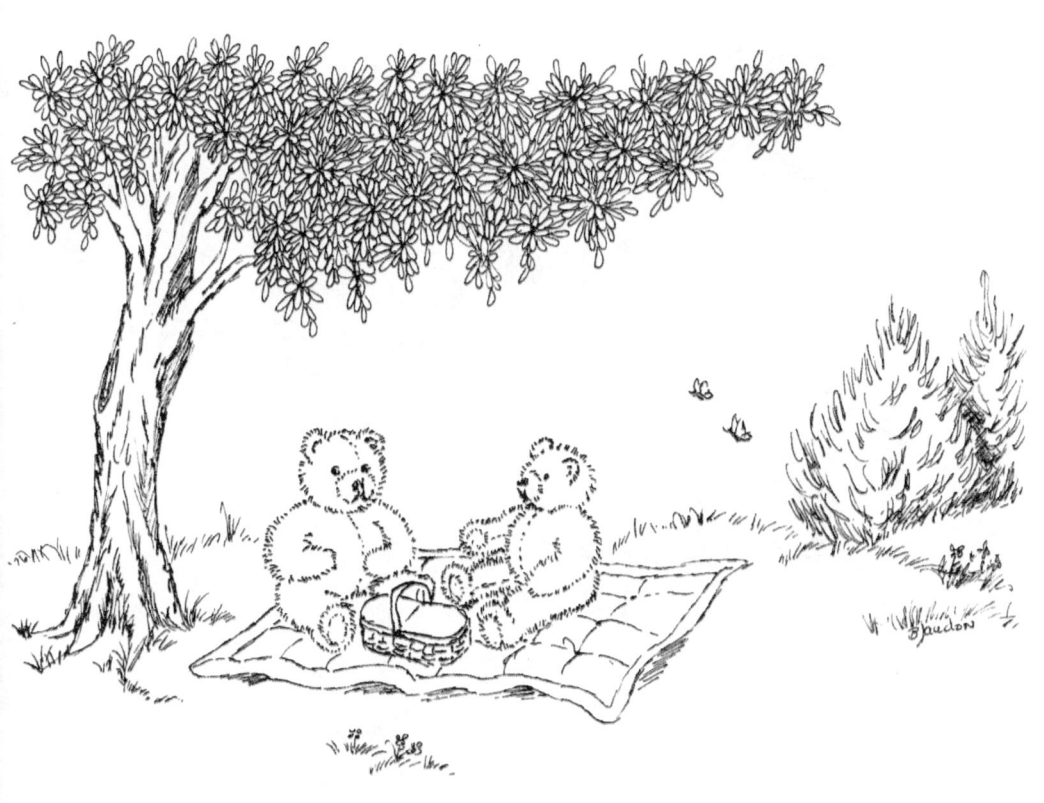

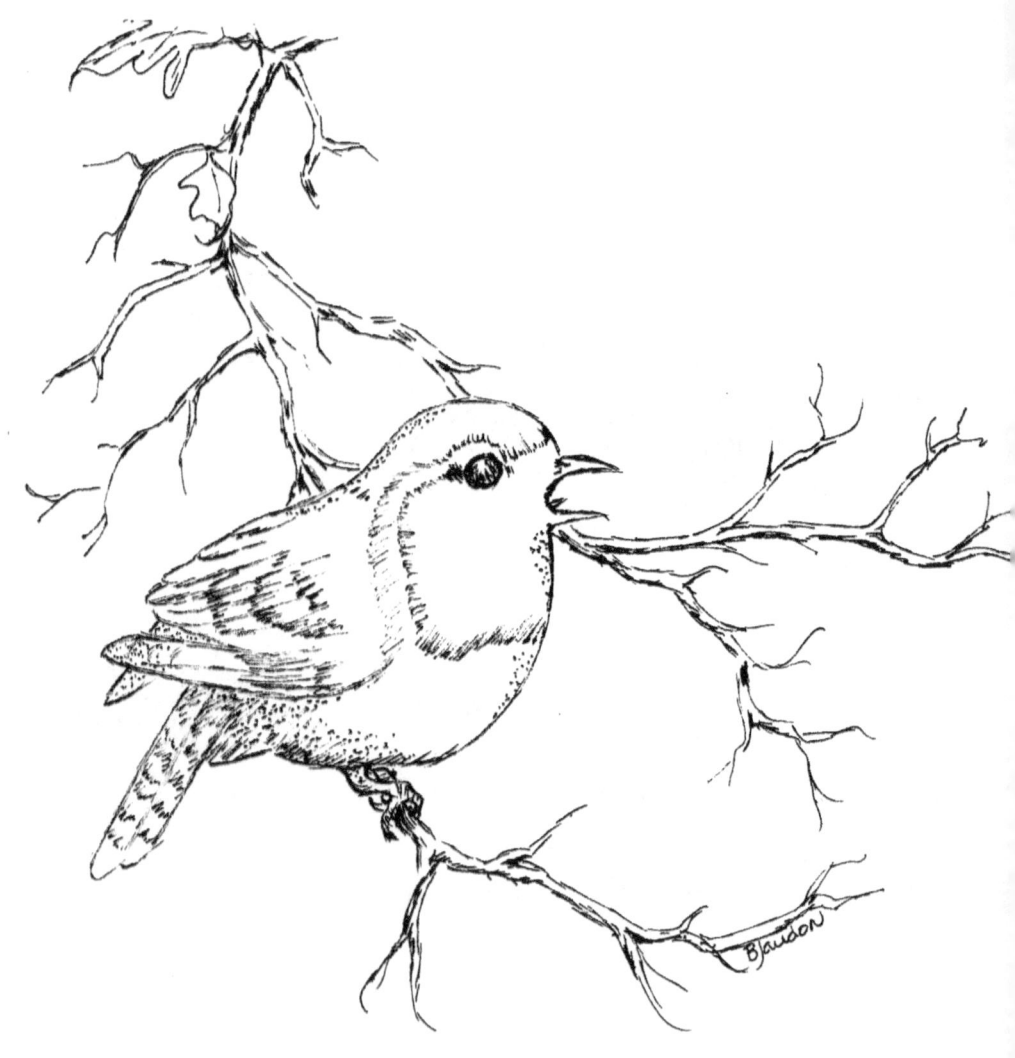

Jerry Bird
September 8, 1999

Joking and laughter,
Now there are seven.
Every time I hold him,
Sure feels like heaven.

Read me 'Squeezy Bug,'
Ten times in a row.
Read again and again,
This time read slow.

Yesterday remember...

Behind you twenty years,
Into the future you run.
Envision twenty more,
Where have they gone?

Remember them with joy,
When the stories are told.
Drop away all sadness,
Keep only the gold.

You're now over forty,
But you're still not that old!
Into the future you run.
This time run slow.

Times Remembered

A quiet place not easily found.
A walk along on leafy ground.
A time to rest the weary mind.
Leaving the cares of the day behind.

You sit alone at the water's edge.
Wind in the trees play with the image.
A line in the water, expectations unsure.
A bob of the pole and a pull on the lure.

Through your hand into the pole and into the deep.
The cares of your world miraculously leap.
As you play with the creature pulling at your hand.
Simpler concerns become a demand.

A joy returns to the heart and the soul.
A simple instrument found in a pole.
Relieving the mind of every care,
As the music for your soul is discovered there.

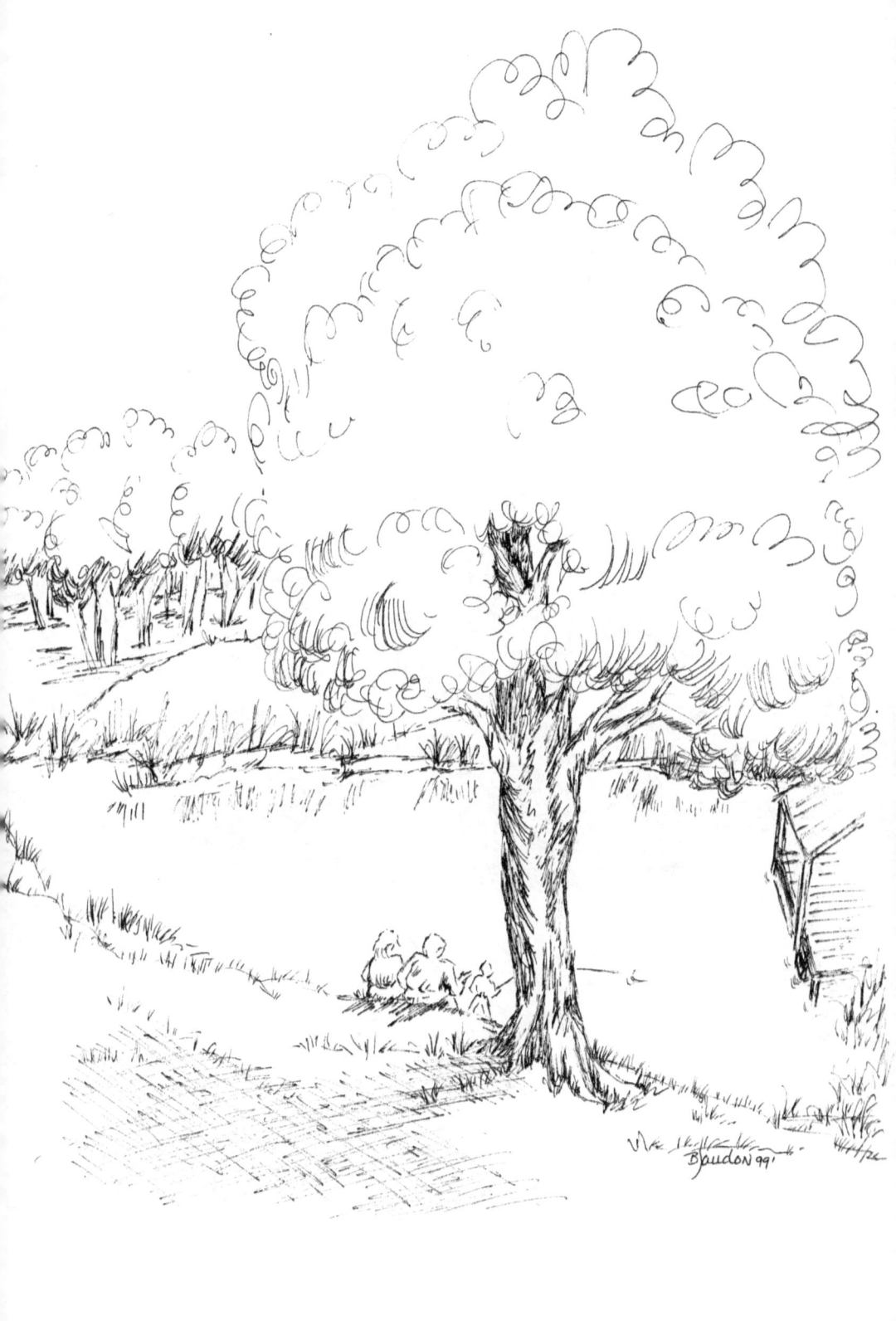

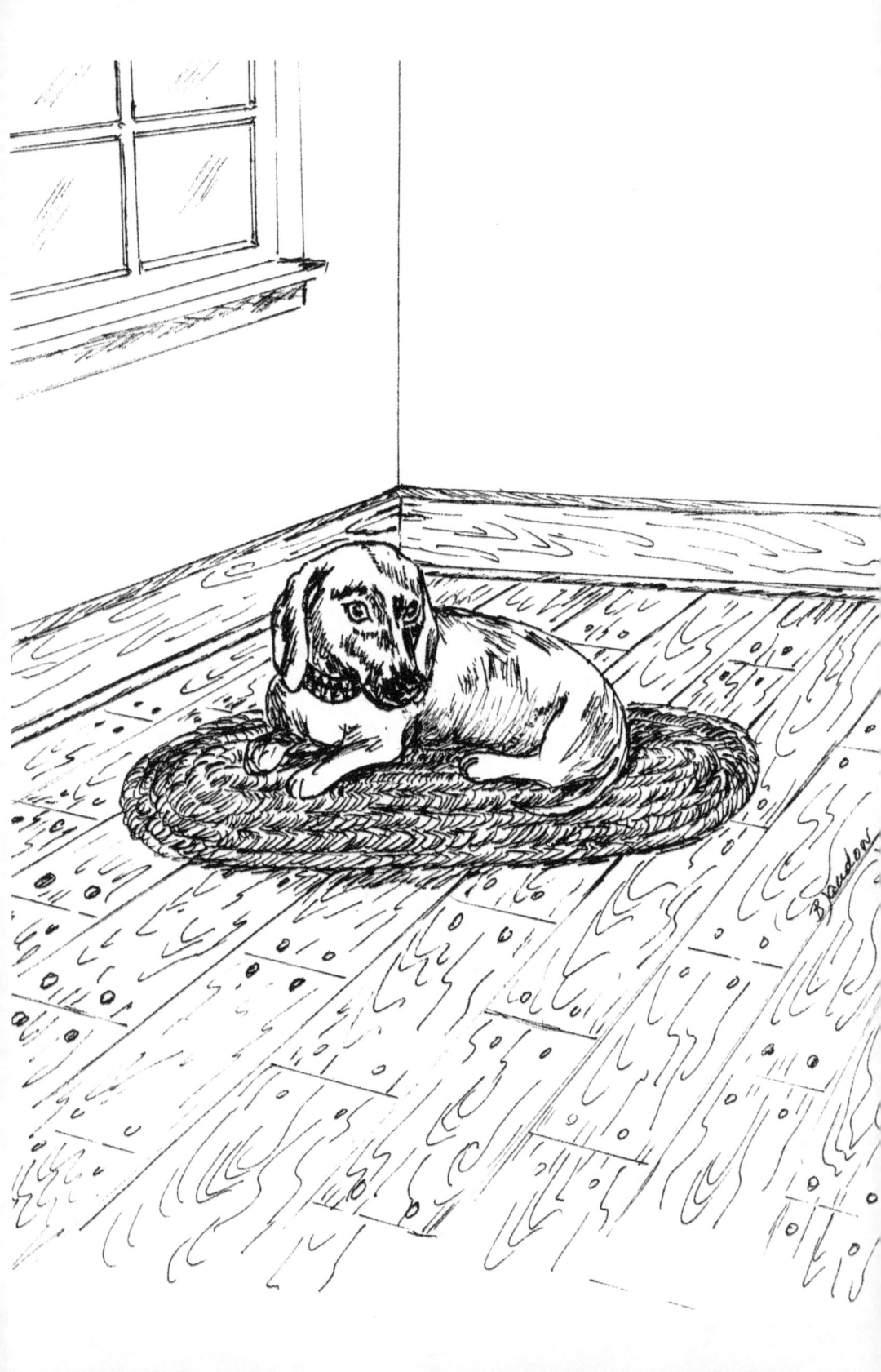

Ode to Brother Jim
August 16, 1999

I'm sending this card.
And a WISH for you.
Hope all your wishes.
This day will come true.

No need to worry.
It's just one more year.
Though a big one it is.
It's still very clear.

You age very well.
The white hair is a killer.
With all those wrinkles.
Still a good lookin' feller.

Friends will remember,
Much more than you care.
Lost items you'll look for.
But they won't be there.

Live it up if you can.
While there is still time.
The other side of this mountain.
Is much harder to climb.

The Journey
April 14, 2001

The journey is planned for us.
In our Father's love entwined.
We struggle vainly then adjust.
To His fruitful purpose we find.

None will know the twists and turns.
In the road we travel along.
The journey is where He helps us learn.
And grow His will as our own.

His plan we know is the perfect one.
Prepared to help us know.
Though we cannot see it clearly.
Our Faith grows stronger as we go.

While on your personal journey.
Take time to embrace each mile.
Your day is just as He planned it.
With purpose, grand design, INTENTIONAL.

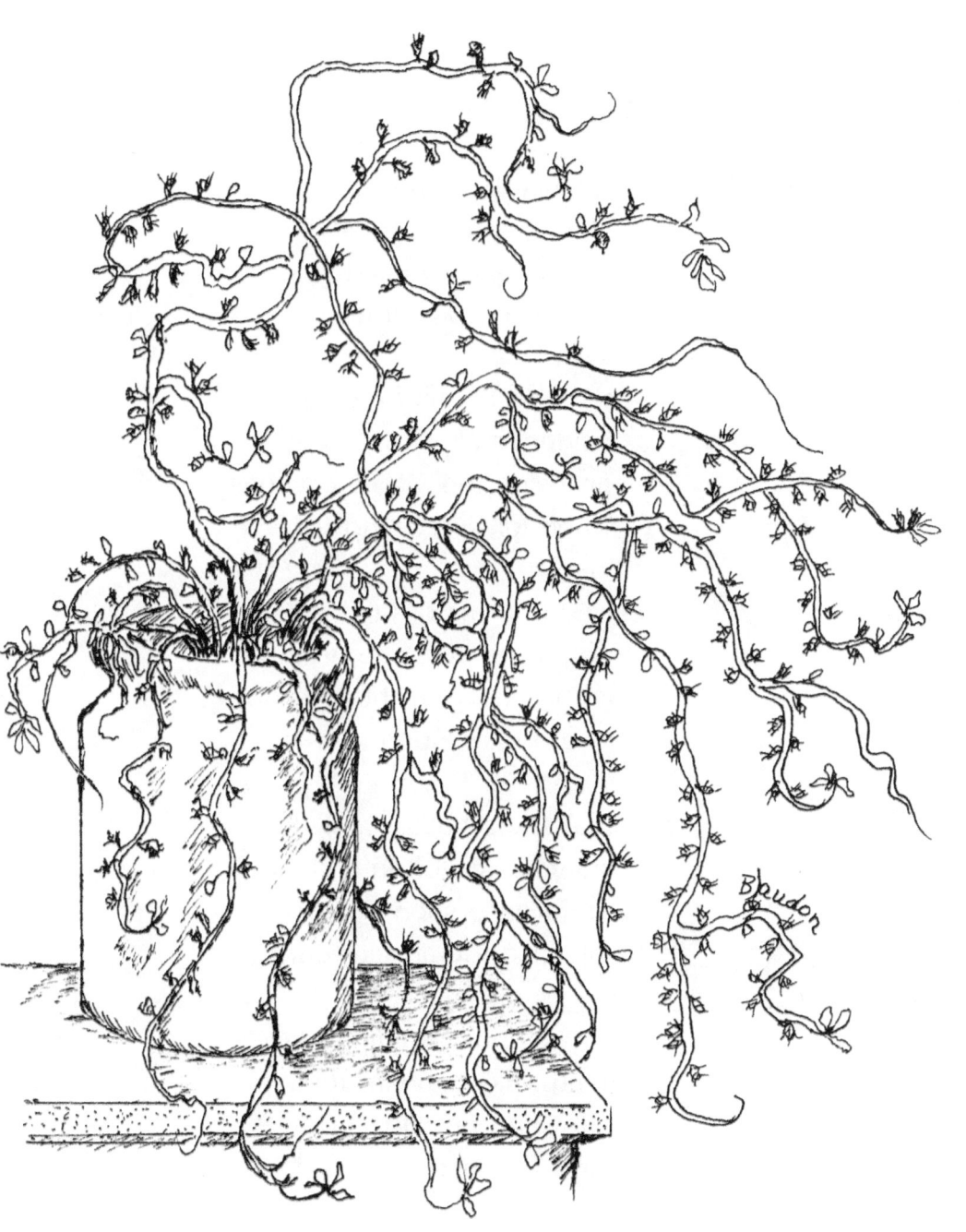

Once Upon A Time

New hearts-empty spaces,
Blank pages not yet inscribed,
Life begins as the fairytales do
Once up a time.

The heart opens expectant,
Tender to all within view,
No fear inside the sterile cocoons,
Excited for everything new.

Relaxed in arms of false safety,
Strong arms gently entwined,
Trusted harbor from the unknown,
For the once upon a time.

Safety may be but a lonely hour,
Destiny has called in a claim,
On innocence soon devoured,
By injustice winning it's game.

Fear has found a hiding place,
Dimming a light meant to shine,
Small world of natural grace,
Began with once upon a time.

No courtroom found for equity,
Nor rally giving voice to the weak,
Nor a giant, imposing formidable,
To save the day, for the prey they seek.

Nor a veiled place from their sight,
Or covering for playful games,
But, a gauntlet of terrible fright,
Deep pools for once upon a time.

Tender fall into silence,
Nothingness flows from deep wounds,
Vast holes tear inside the fences
Until screams like lost souls marooned.

Exposure, like a script in a play,
The stage of the world will see,
Swift is the hand of Judgment Day,
Making right all the inequities.

Fire brings new life from the ashes,
Strength reborn in bright light of day,
True safety and the light clashes,
Once upon a time fades away.

Second Harvest

Summer, once filled with promise,
Spectacular passing discloses a slight hint.
Of fields dressed in rainbows of color,
Labors rewarded from energy long spent.

The scent of fall floats in the air,
Adrift on a crisp, cool breezes.
The wind plays a familiar tune,
Through sun-dried leaves and grasses.

Harvest time grows from what is done,
See withered stalks brown and bent.
The breeze inspires a leisurely yawn,
That echoes this marvelous event.

Second Harvest fill up empty spaces,
Young artist admire them big and small.
Then carve into orange glaring faces,
A small yellow flame tells all.

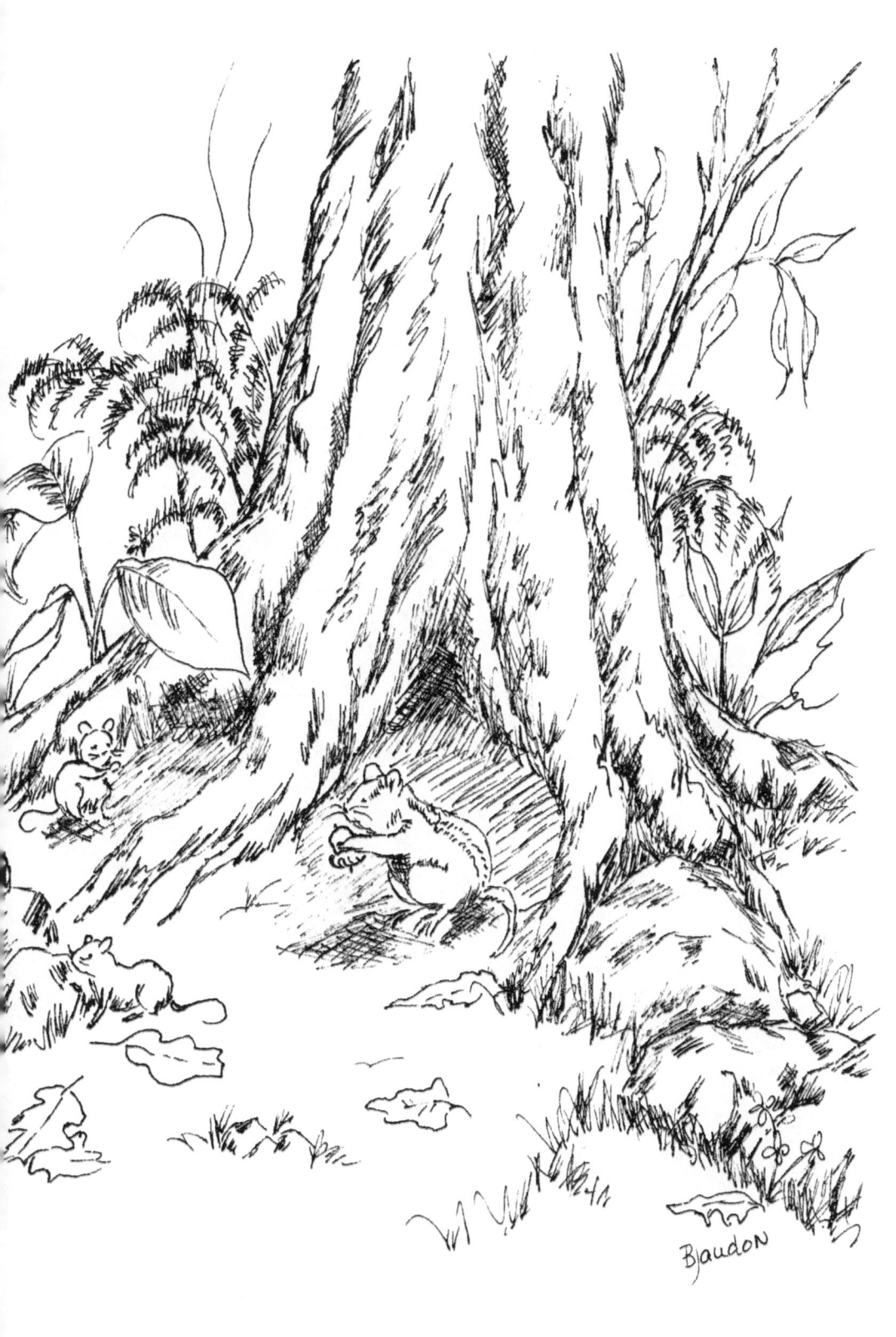

Blaudon

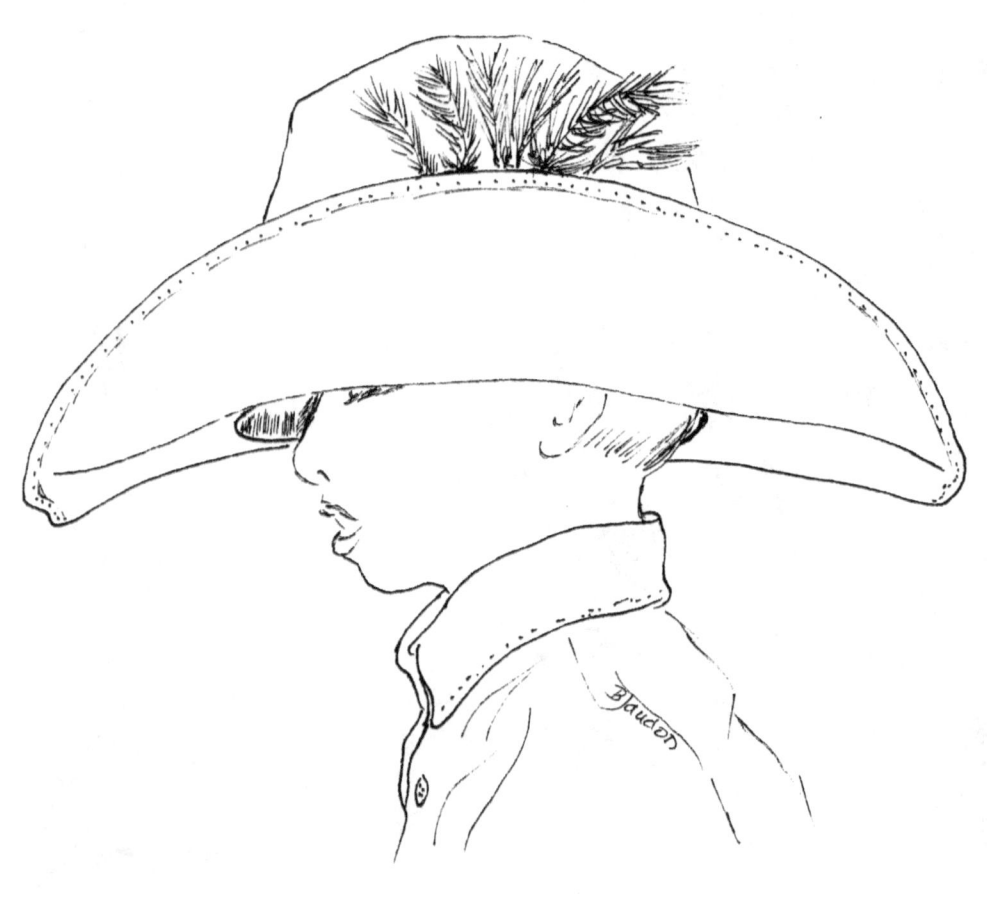

Fall On Fire
April 2009

Cool wind replays an old noisy tune,
Through grass and dry leaves blended.
The music calls out to the harvest moon,
Surrounded by stars hung suspended.

Earth's morning canvas stands ablaze,
Splash a pallet into breathtaking wonder.
Amber and gold luminous displays,
Fall's signature in magnificent splendor.

Ageless harmony in rhythm of old,
The eyes are wide in awe of the vision.
Plays to the same tune ever so bold,
Fleeting the glory once held in suspension.

The Winding Road
February 24, 2000

All must take the winding road,
That will lead us to our dreams.
Of finding love and family so,
Time holds more than what it seems.

As once upon your perfect day,
More than forty-three years ago,
Two lovers wed and all still say,
'They love each other so.'

Your family grew, once two - now eight,
So designed for you from above.
Loving hearts no longer must they wait,
For a God centered home grounded in love.

Our birthday wish for you Mother dear,
Pouring from hearts proud and true.
Our home is 'HOME' because you are here,
We thank God for blessing us with you.

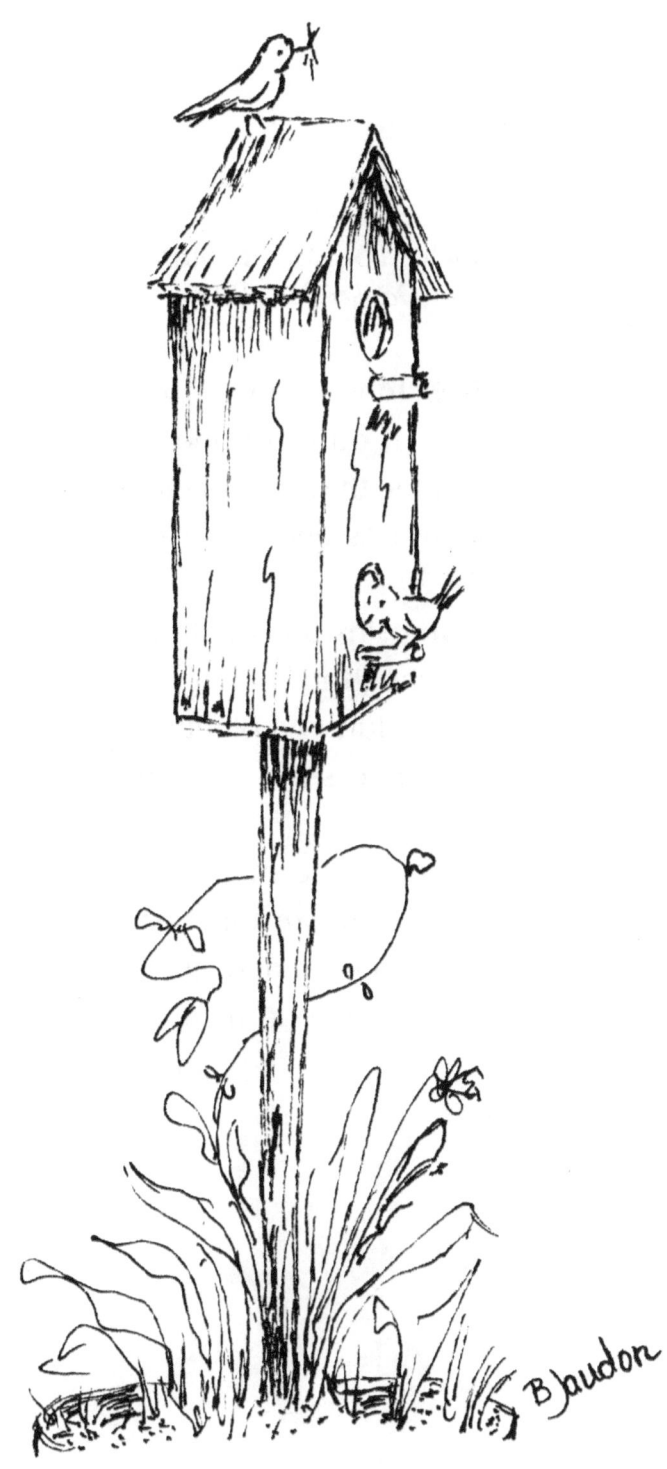

Blaudon

Ode To Sister Mary
October 31, 1999

Oh, October - Oh, October
What do you bring?
Weather that turns colder.
The spooks and Holloween.

The pumpkins are made ready.
To laugh in the night.
The fun is a-plenty.
The spooks are a fright.

We look at the many faces,
Now who can this be?
Cat-like moves and graces,
Its gotta be our Ma-a-a-ry.

Some might be so sad
About the many years plus.
Just makes her so glad.
What's all the fuss?

The sparkle in her eye.
Ready smile-toothy grin.
Not one will deny.
A Youthful Spirit found within.

She gets into the Spirit
With the spooks and the shrills.
A National Holiday declare it.
Mary's Birthday and we're THRILLED!

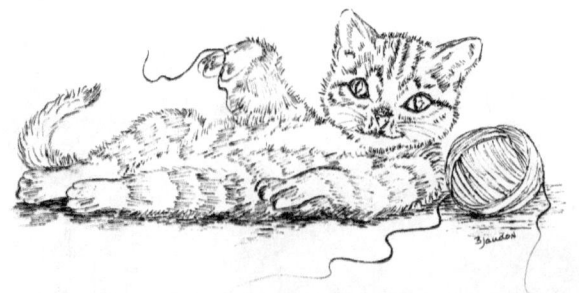

Winter

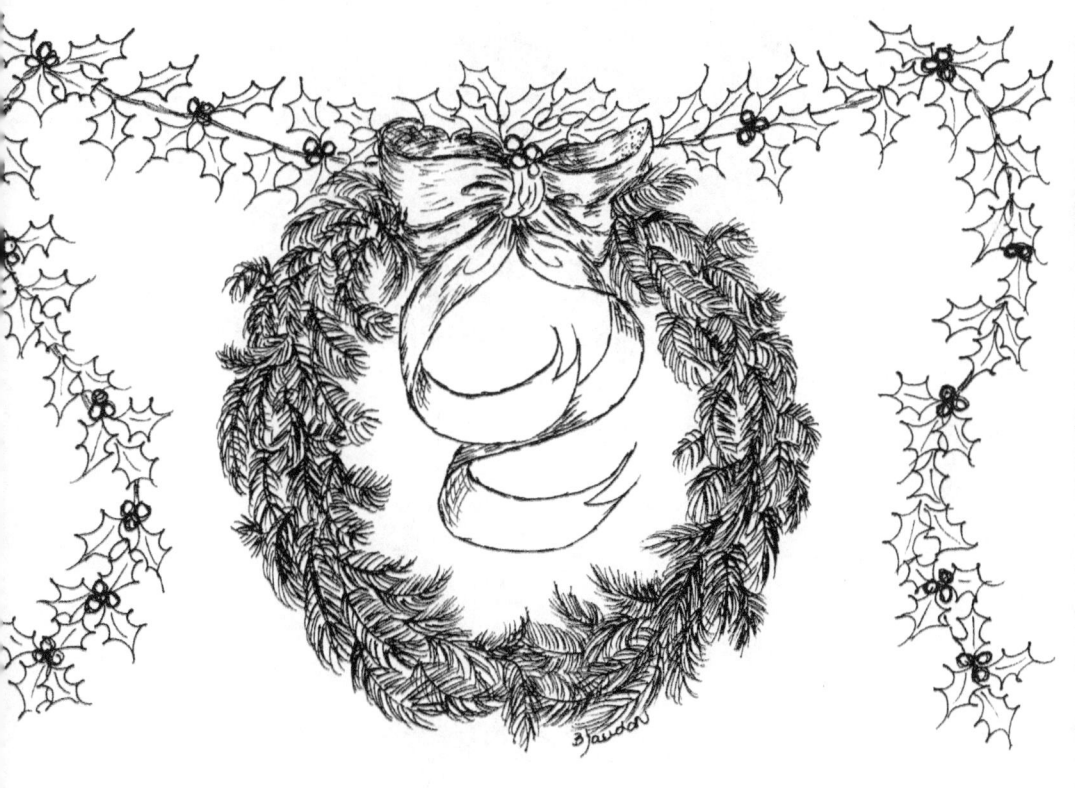

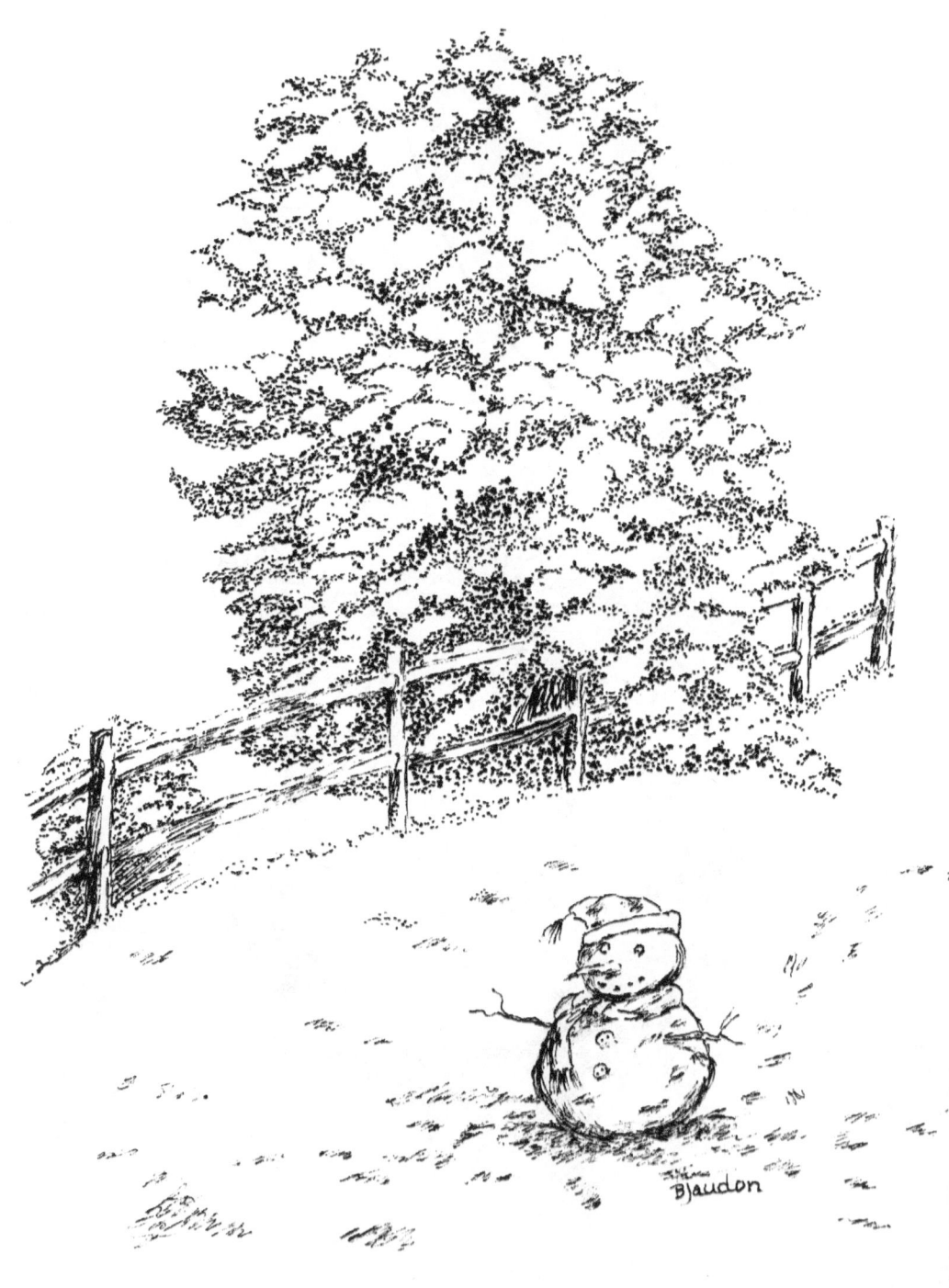

Snow
August 1, 2023

Can you feel it?
How the wind brushes your nose.
Can you feel it?
As Fall comes to a close.

Can you see it?
In the trees. fields and grasses.
Can you see it?
In the colors-as a chill advances.

Can you hear it?
In the melody of a lonely voice calling.
Can you hear it!
In the last acorn falling.

Can you feel it?
When a chill bites at your nose.
Can you feel it?
Wind tossing your hair and clothes.

Can you hear it!
In a lonely voice calling.
Ahh Winter. I can see it.
The beauty in the first snowflake falling.

Father Time

Mother Nature and Father Time,
Join together to make a rhyme.

The hands of time keep turning around,
No way to stop them has ever been found.

Each person is given one place in time,
To create the formula and unique design.

How well we construct the forms on the page,
Developed along with the markers of age.

When it is time to place the last line,
The world will see clearly a life well defined.

My prayer is heaven will see beauty unfold,
When the joy, laughter, and peace of your story is told.

Mother Nature and Father Time,
Join together to make a rhyme.

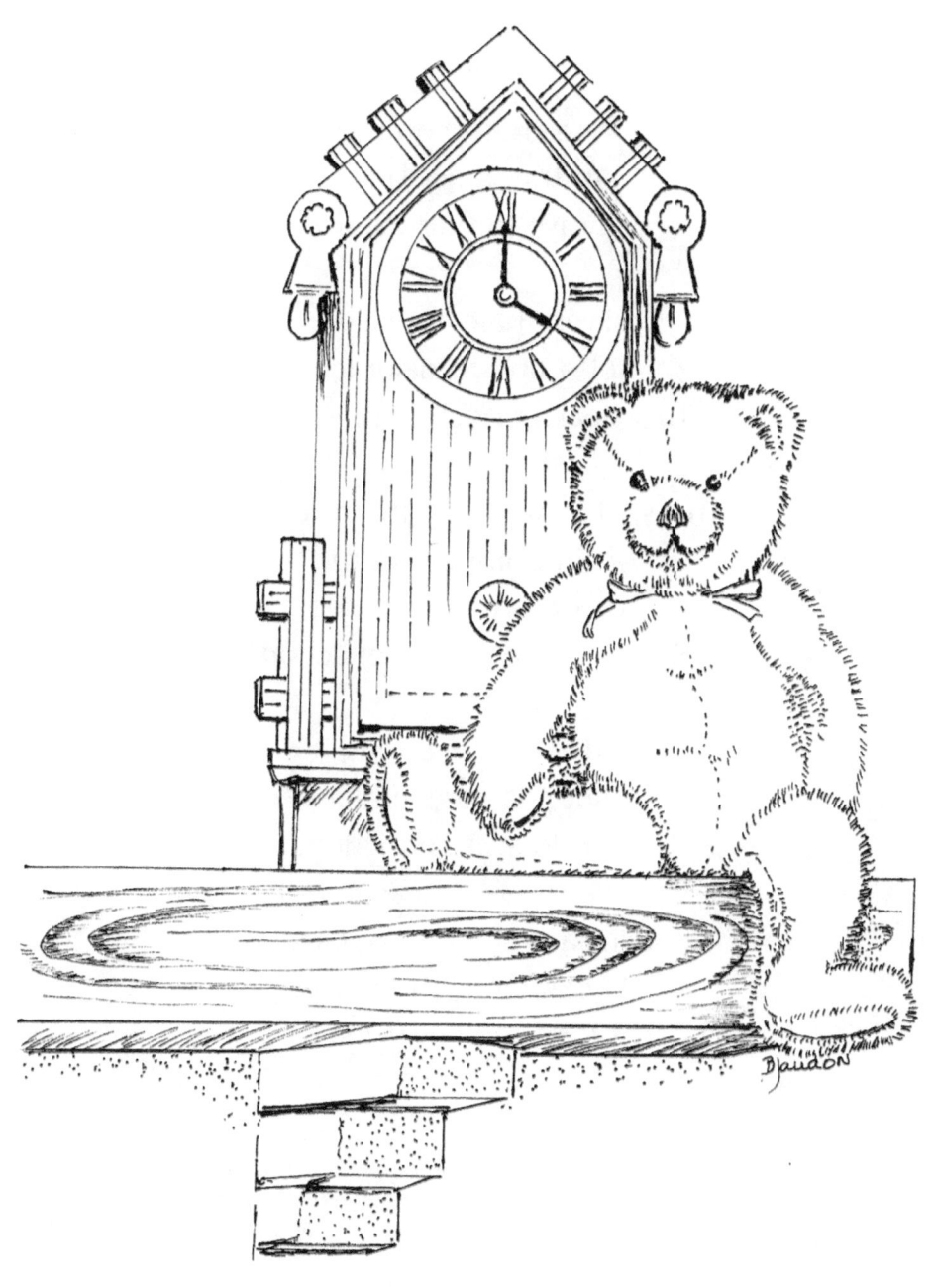

Paper Dolly's

We dress so fine.
In the latest kind.
Always to perfection.

Every hair in place.
Not a line to disgrace.
This near perfect complexion.

That's what we want them to see.
Not the imperfect me.
For we are all you see.
Showing the same reflection.

My voice is strong.
It sounds so confident.
With lots of conviction.

With a smile on my face.
My confidence in place.
I look so convincing.

We aren't what we seem to be,
There's only the imperfect to me.
After all we are you see,
Showing the same reflection.

Why can't we show,
All that we really know,
Not just the expected.

Its so hard to be,
Only what others see.
The real me is neglected.

I'm not that strong you see,
Inside is the imperfect me,
And I will always be.

Paper Dolly's, Paper Dolly's,
Aren't perfect you can see,
They are wrinkled and broken like me.

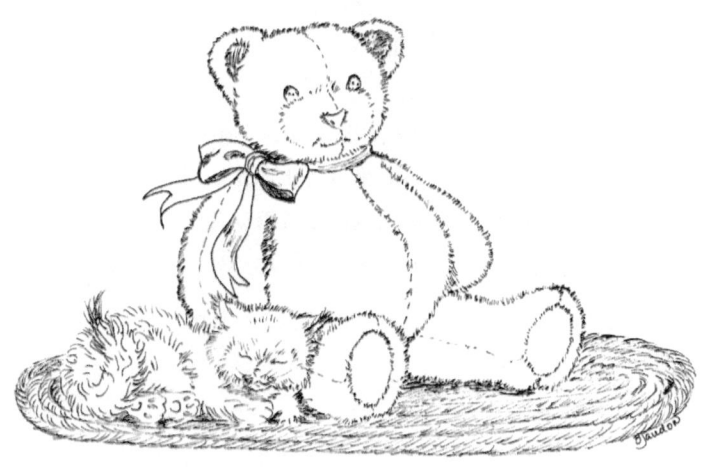

Missed You at the Reunion

Outstanding group from the past.
Each one turned out to be.
Arriving, still in perfect form.
Wish you could have seen.

Each hair in place.
Those shapes still shapely.
Not one gray hair found.
Recognition was easy.

Where have we been?
Where are we now?
This group turned out perfect.
As the video will avow.

New memories were made.
Until we meet once again.
We still want to see you.
Sonny will tell you when.

A reunion like this one.
Can rarely be found.
The dynamic group from '59.
Was the best one in town.

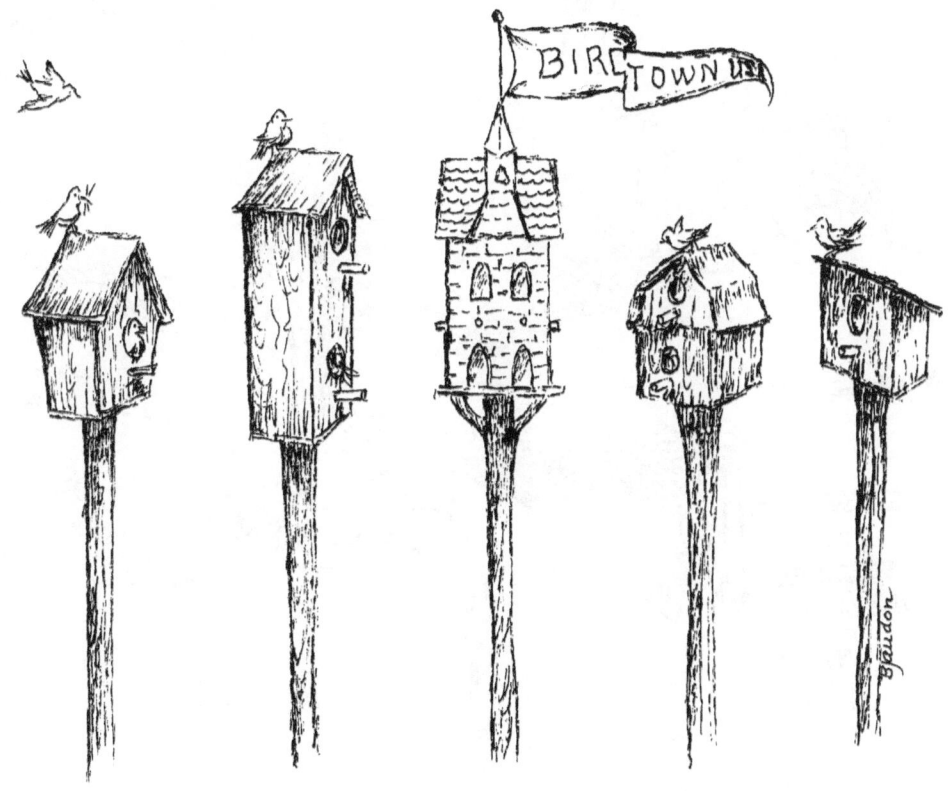

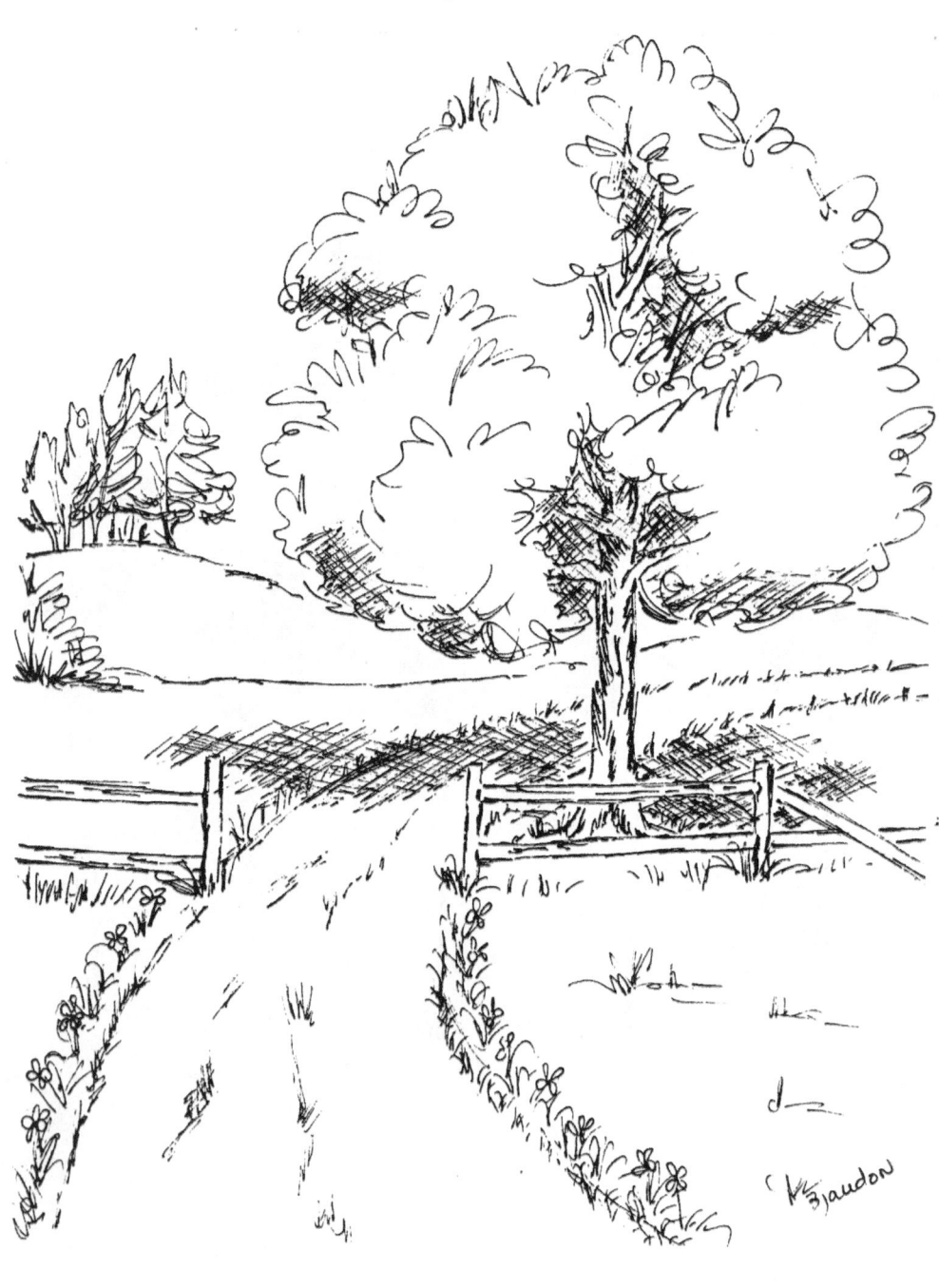

Reflections

There is a place within the heart,
The spirit walks alone.
To rest the mind and set it free,
To think of times long gone.

I set my mind on a quiet place,
Leave care and worry behind.
Refresh my soul with peaceful thoughts,
And feel myself unwind.

The lane is long and winding,
stretched beyond my view.
Lined with trees and shadows,
The fragrance of earth and dew.

My spirit begins to wander,
Lifting high upon the wind.
Giving wings to my weary footsteps,
Renewed spirit HE plants within.

Ah, I revel in this moment,
Too soon I must let it go,
And return to my place of service,
Reflecting, refreshed, and aglow.

Winter
April, 14, 2009

While we slept a white veil has fallen on creation.
See the ghostly forms under a mountain of drift.
Young and old greet the timeless invitation.
Design a snow angel on white wings uplifted.

Unique inspiration does each season give way.
Flamboyant expression fall upon each new day.
The Master's brush-strokes across all creation.
His Glory for our pleasure is on display.

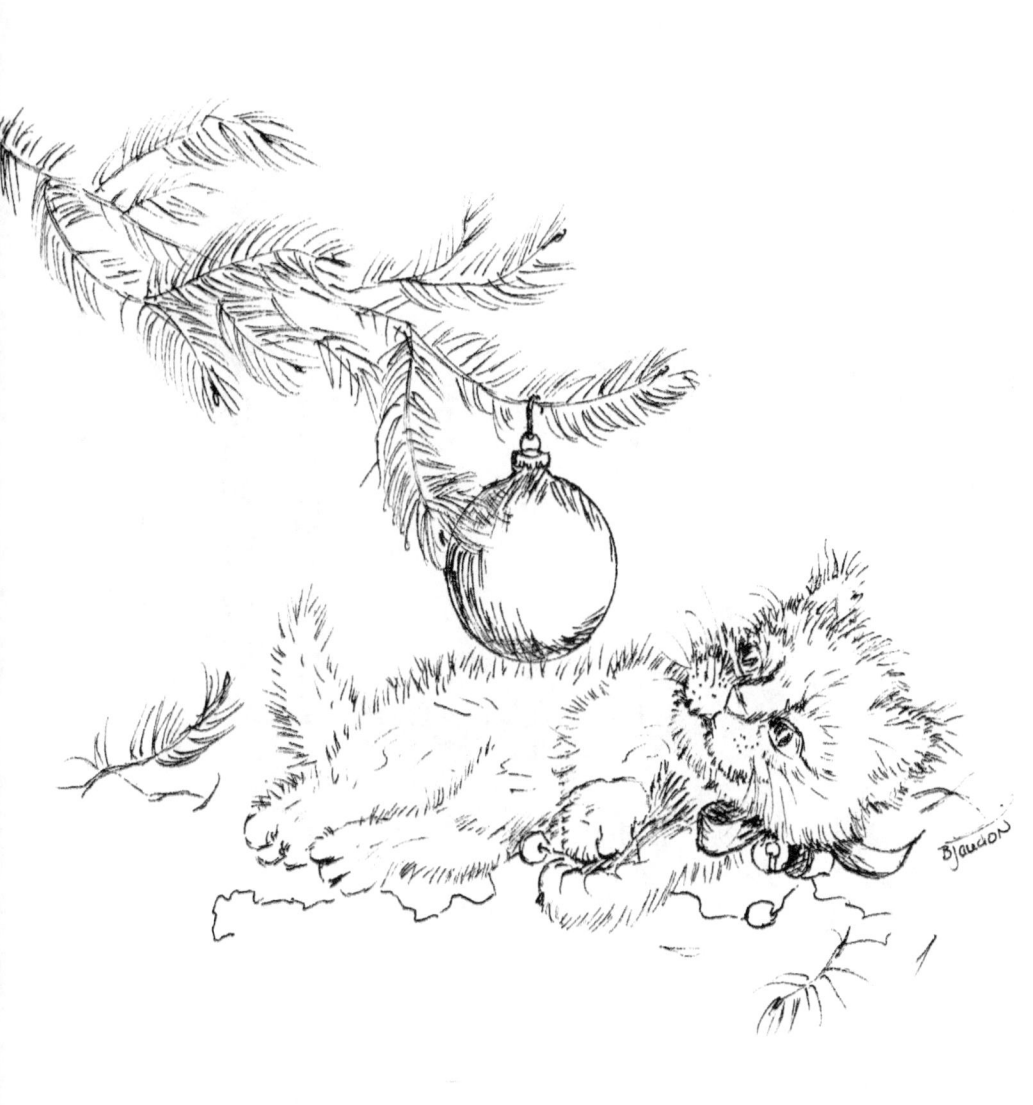

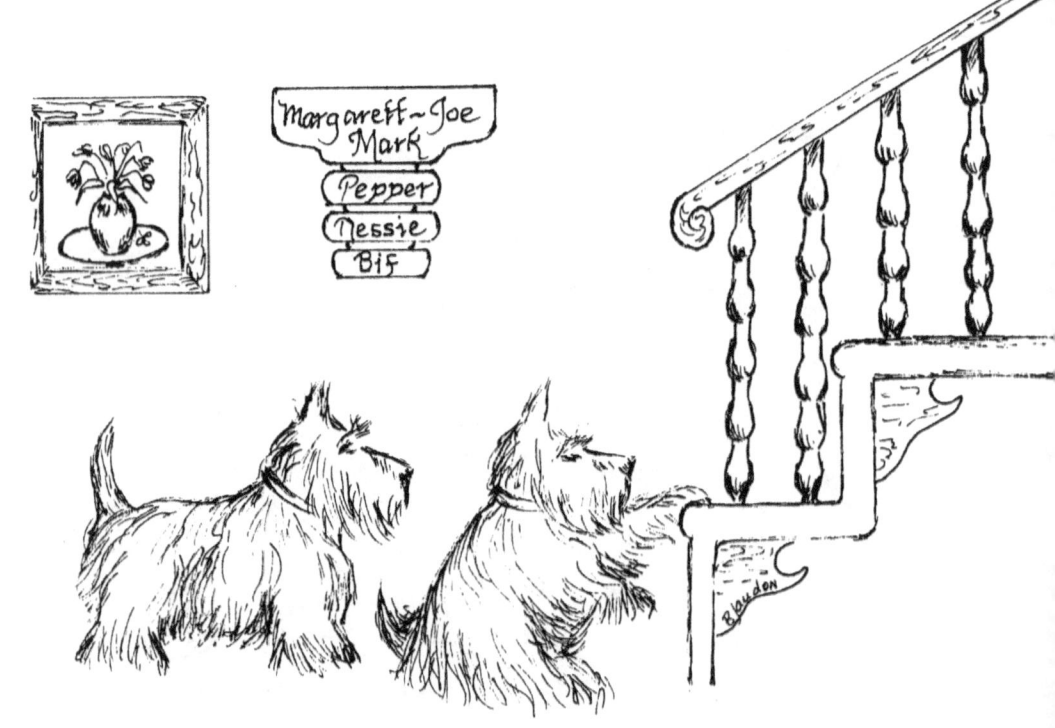

Margaret~Joe
Mark
Pepper
Nessie
Bif

Bloudon

A Sister Is
August 3, 2023

A Sister is...

The one who listens to my mistakes.
Promising there will be a better day ahead.

The one who calls me,
Encouraging though life has played a nasty trick.

The one I share with,
Joys that call for a celebration with more than one.

The one who lets me,
Lean for a little while when the load gets heavy.

The one who in a emotional moment,
Understands without me saying a single word.

The one in the midst of flops and failures,
Laughs with me through sloppy tears.

The one who hears and
keeps my deepest and darkest secrets.

The one who loves me
Unconditionally no matter the wounds of time.

A Sister is...
One of God's riches blessings.

I thank God for my sisters' each one-
Margaret, Mary, Judy, and our Elizabeth.

Where Do They Go?
April, 10, 2009

Where Do They Go?
Face pressed to the window.
Droplets glide down the pane.
See, the rain is crying.
See the water so slowly.
Winding on the windowpane.
Mommy, mommy.
Where do they go?
When it's raining.
Or lots of snow.
It's wet out there.
How can they fly?
Where is home
Up in the sky?
Where is warm.
Or wings to hold them.
Where is soft.
Who will keep them safe?
When winds blow cold.
Or skies are dark.
Who gives love?
To the Meadow Lark?
When there is rain and snow.

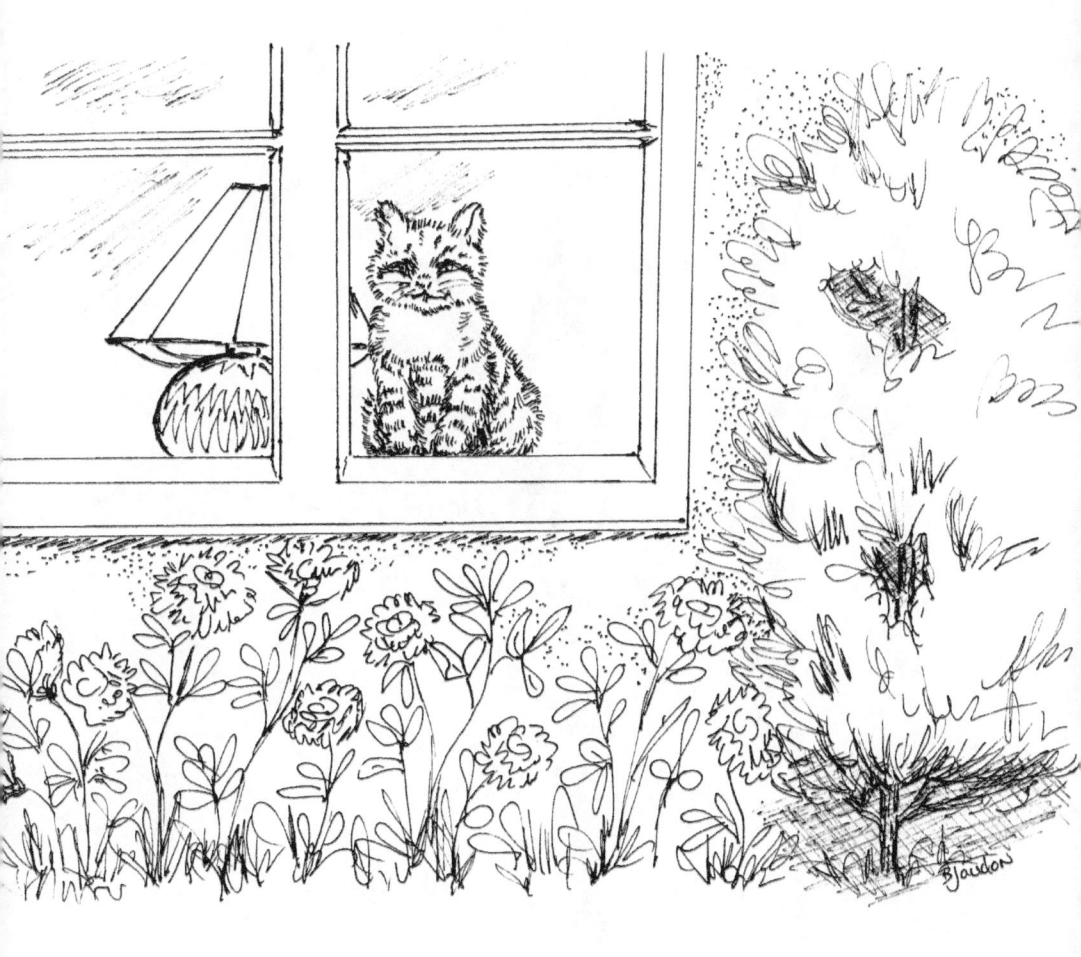

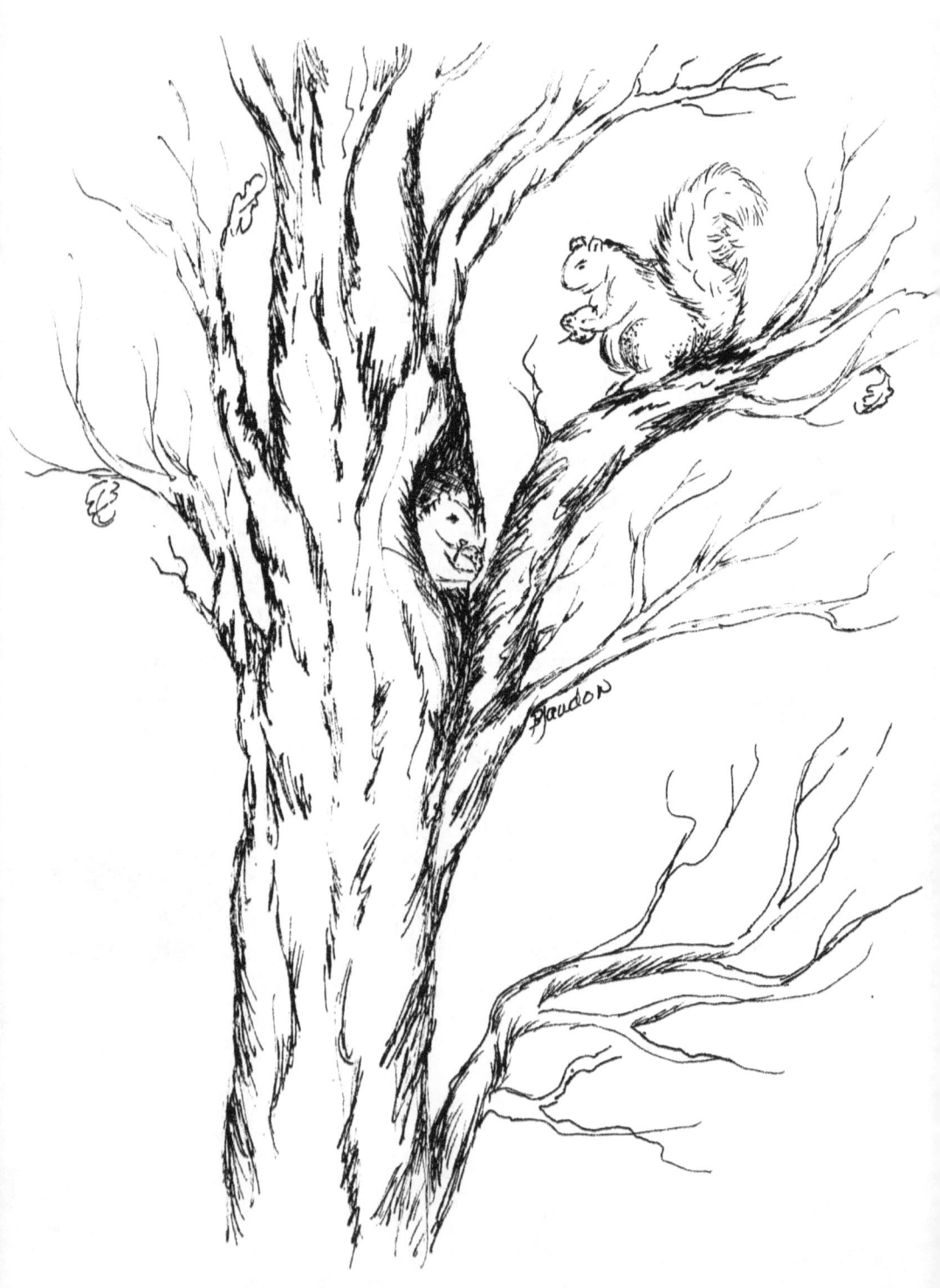

Storm Clouds
April 10, 2009

I see a storm cloud brewing,
Where do the critters go?
Under a tree log, a bush, or in a hole
Or, in a bunker with a blind mole?

I see the birds are flying,
They need a safe place, too.
High in a tree, not on the ground,
Like other critters do.

A home out from harms way,
From the cold rain or snow.
A dry place for resting,
From the cold winds that blow.

I see a storm cloud brewing,
Where do the critters go?

Dear Cathleen
January 1, 2008

Oh, the years have flown away,
Like rose petals on the wind.
The comfort that my arms did sway,
Are open as your friend.

Look at you now, my dear,
Young lady no longer alone.
Your heart doesn't need my care,
Challenges you have bravely won.

Confidence! You have discovered,
In your fresh bloom of youth,
Open to what is yet undelivered,
Freedom inhaled on each breath.

Those fragile times of worry,
Echo in the halls of your past,
Where you visit hurriedly,
Reflecting and sifting the chafe.

Time will censor the imagined,
Wisdom your reality wash clear.
The hall of memories well lighted,
Age softens them year after year.

The breadth of your life unfolding,
Especially blended into mine.
Precious, valued, remolded,
My own child by God's design.

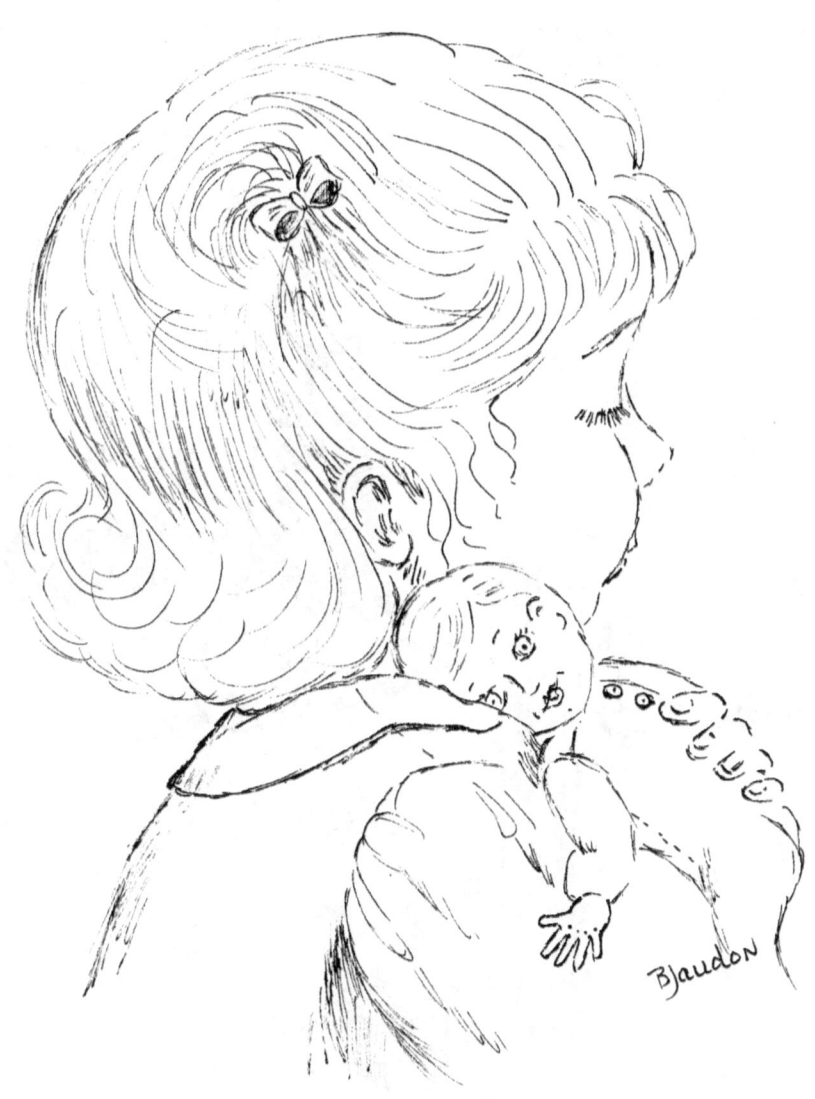

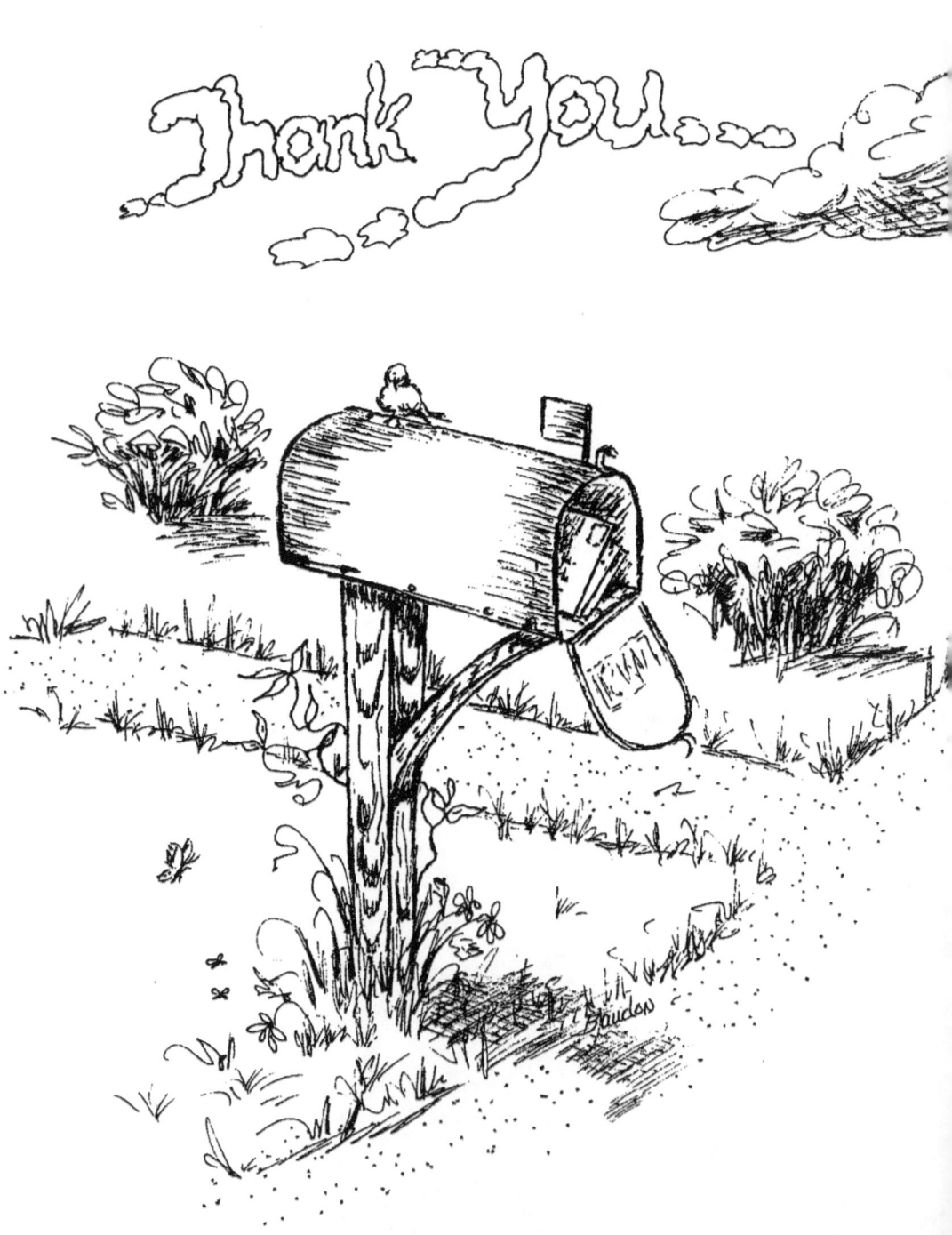

A Journey

There is a journey planned for us,
By our Father loving and kind.
We struggle vainly then adjust,
His purpose is what we find.

None will know the twists and turns,
That life will take us on.
The journey is meant to help us learn,
And make His will our own.

His plan, we know, is a perfect one,
Prepared to help us grow.
Though we cannot see it today,
When we are troubled so.

While on your winding journey,
Take time to rest awhile.
The comfort comes from learning,
HE is with you in every trial.

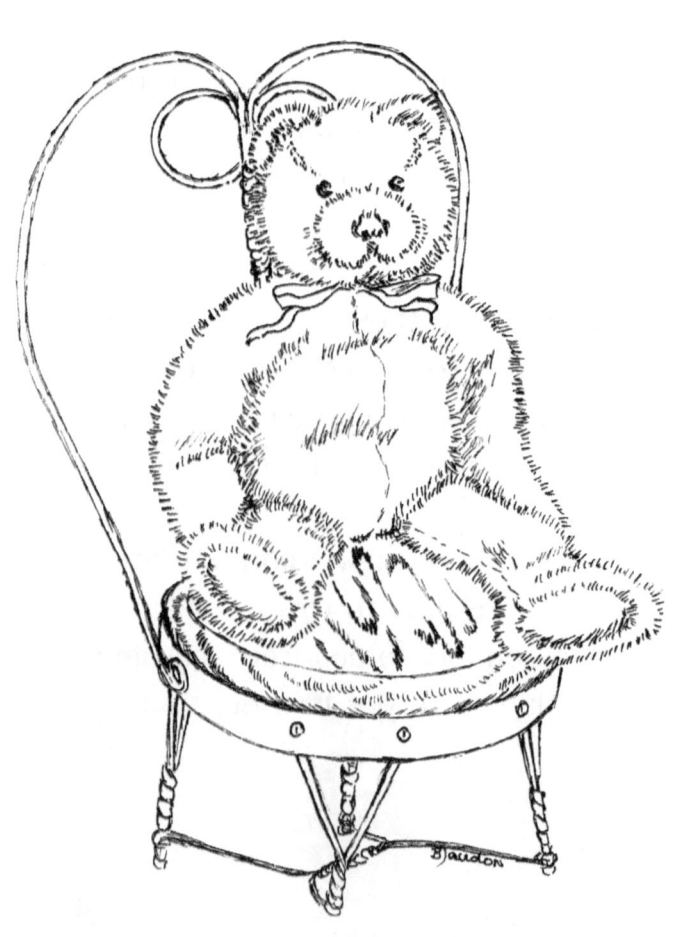

www.ingramcontent.com/pod-product-compliance
Lightning Source LLC
Chambersburg PA
CBHW022343290526
45786CB00014B/2386